~ SPURGEON ~

THE $\mathcal{P}$OWER OF CHRIST'S TEARS

Dear Felix

" The Lord will open the heavens,
the storehouse of His bounty,
to send rain on your land in
season and to bless all the
work of your hands.. "
(Deuteronomy 28:12)

CLC
CHRISTIAN ~ LIVING ~ CLASSICS

In Him
Gary & Nelly

On your graduation, May 99

CHARLES SPURGEON

Christian Living Classics

THE POWER OF CHRIST'S TEARS

Compiled and Edited by LANCE WUBBELS

Emerald Books

P.O. Box 635
Lynnwood, Washington 98046

Scripture quotations are taken from the King James Version of the Bible.

About the Author

CHARLES HADDON SPURGEON (1834–1892) was the remarkable British "Boy Preacher of the Fens" who became one of the truly greatest preachers of all time. Coming from a flourishing country pastorate in 1854, he accepted a call to pastor London's New Park Street Chapel. This building soon proved too small and so work on Spurgeon's Metropolitan Tabernacle was begun in 1859. Meanwhile his weekly sermons were being printed and having a remarkable sale—25,000 copies every week in 1865 and translated into more than twenty languages.

Spurgeon built the Metropolitan Tabernacle into a congregation of over 6,000 and added well over 14,000 members during his thirty-eight-year London ministry. The combination of his clear voice, his mastery of language, his sure grasp of Scripture, and a deep love for Christ produced some of the noblest preaching of any age. An astounding 3,561 sermons have been preserved in sixty-three volumes, *The New Park Street Pulpit* and *The Metropolitan Tabernacle Pulpit*, from which the chapters of this book have been selected and edited.

During his lifetime, Spurgeon is estimated to have preached to 10,000,000 people. He remains history's most widely read preacher. There is more available material written by Spurgeon than by any other Christian author, living or dead. His sixty-three volumes of sermons stand as the largest set of books by a single author in the history of Christianity, comprising the equivalent to the twenty-seven volumes of the ninth edition of the *Encyclopedia Britannica*.

About the Editor

LANCE WUBBELS is the managing editor of Bethany House Publishers. His interest in the writings of Charles Spurgeon began while doing research on an editorial project that required extensive reading of Spurgeon's sermons. He discovered a wealth of sermon classics that are filled with practical, biblical insight for every believer and written in a timeless manner that makes them as relevant today as the day they were spoken. His desire is to select and present Spurgeon's writings in a way that will appeal to a wide audience of readers and allow one of the greatest preachers of all time to enrich believers' lives.

Wubbels is the author of *The Gentle Hills* fiction series with Bethany House Publishers, a four-book series that is set during World War II, as well as the heartwarming short novel, *One Small Miracle*. A naturally gifted storyteller, he captures readers with a warm, homey style filled with wit and insight that appeals to a wide readership.

Contents

Introduction

ONE CANNOT STUDY THE LIFE of Jesus Christ without being struck by the intense passions that coursed through the soul of our great Lord and Master. That He was "the man of sorrows and acquainted with grief," as the prophet Isaiah so vividly described Him in his classic fifty-third chapter, and that the Savior lived out those words in His daily life, is the fascinating subject of this book. And who better to expound on this theme than Charles Spurgeon, the legendary English Baptist preacher.

Spanning nearly four decades of pastoral and evangelistic ministry in the city of London during the second half of the nineteenth century, Spurgeon's passionate biblical expositing transformed the lives of thousands of listeners as he addressed the deepest needs of the human heart. Centering his preaching around the person of Jesus Christ, Spurgeon built London's Metropolitan Tabernacle into the world's largest independent congregation. His preaching legacy may never be surpassed, and as the epitomy of pulpit mastery, he astonished his generation with sermons so thoroughly grounded in biblical doctrine and so insightful into the human condition that they bear a timeless trait that supersedes the era in which they were given.

As a man of great personal passion himself, Charles Spurgeon preached with a sense of wonderment as he considered those passages of Scripture that describe Jesus when He was deeply moved in His emotions. Indignation, compassion, grief, tenderness, sorrow, sympathy, lamentation, anger, and agony are only some of the passions that we see in Jesus' life. And those intense emotions caused Him to take action and are immeasurably instructive for those who desire to follow Him as disciples.

On three biblical occasions we are told that Jesus wept. The first was at the grave of Lazarus, where the tears of Jesus were so intense that the stunned Jewish onlookers said, "Behold how he loved him!" He saw the sorrow of the sisters and stood face to face with the last enemy, death, and groaned in spirit over the fruit of sin in the death and corruption of the body, and then we are told that "Jesus wept." Let these two words stand in solitary sublimity and simplicity, for they contain a world of healing balm condensed into a single drop. To understand something of the Savior's sorrow over a friend and how He sanctified the tears of the bereaved is a great comfort in the life of any believer.

The second recording of Jesus' tears came when our Lord beheld the beloved city of Jerusalem and wept over it, foreseeing as a prophet the judgments that would come upon the rebellious city. His deep lament that He would have gathered the city to Himself as a hen gathers her chicks is expressed by signs of woe and by words that showed how bitter was His grief. His distress at the evils that awaited His countrymen challenges our hearts to seek the lost and perishing.

The third occasion is recorded in Hebrews 5 and speaks of "the Gethsemane agony, in which a shower of bitter tears was mingled with the bloody sweat." Here we find that Jesus' weeping was induced by the great burden of human guilt that pressed upon Him. "The strength of His love strove with the anguish of His soul and, in the process, forced forth the sacred waters of His eyes." This shows us how we, too, should look upon the guilt of men and mourn over it before God.

Then we follow Spurgeon as he goes on to consider some of other great passages of Scripture that give us a wider picture of the heart of Jesus Christ. To catch a glimpse of the compassion that stirred within Jesus as He viewed the hungry multitude should stir us to consider how we might get involved with feeding the world around us with Christ's redemptive gospel. To know that we have a great High Priest who has suffered Himself and sympathizes with us in every way and is able to comfort our hearts reaches into the depths of our lives. To comprehend that Jesus is the meek and lowly One and that we may come to Him and that He is grieved when we fail to come is wonderful news to our troubled hearts. To understand the gentleness of Jesus, even toward those who hated Him, builds our confidence to come before the Father's throne with boldness. And yet when we see His anger toward hypocrisy and hardness of heart, it should cause us to rid ourselves of all that prevents His light from shining into our lives.

I invite you to read these twelve select chapters as you would listen to a trusted and skilled pastor. There is nothing speculative about Spurgeon's teaching; just the rock-solid truth. Spurgeon will meet you where you live, and you will not be disappointed.

Careful editing has helped to sharpen the focus of these sermons while retaining the authentic and timeless flavor they undoubtedly bring.

*J*esus wept"; He was not ashamed to acknowledge the affliction that sin caused to His holy soul nor the gash that the sight of death made in His heart. He could not bear to see the grave and its corruption. May we never think of the sin and misery of our race without sorrow! I confess I can never go through this huge city of London without feeling unhappy. I never pass from end to end without feeling a black and dark cloud hanging like a pall over my spirit. How my heart breaks for you, O sinful city of London! Is it not so you? What do you feel as you confront sin, poverty, ungodliness, drunkenness, and vice in the streets? These may well go through a man's heart like sharp swords. How Jesus would have wept over my great city! He could not stand in front of a lone grave, about to look upon a single corpse, without weeping. He saw in that one death the representation of what sin has done on so enormous a scale that it is impossible to compute the devastation, and therefore He wept. What have you not done, O Sin! You have slain all these, O Death! What a field of blood has Satan made this earth! The Savior could not stand unmoved in the presence of the destroyer or approach the gate of death's palace without deep emotion. Of this He was by no means ashamed. Holy emotion is not a weakness. If at any time in the midst of the world's wickedness and celebration you weep, do not hide those tears! Let the thoughtless see that there is one, at least, who fears God and trembles when the Holy One is provoked.

Chapter One

Jesus Wept

Jesus wept—John 11:35.

A GREAT STORM WAS STIRRING the mind of Jesus. We find, when looking at the original, that He was indignant and troubled. We have a very literal translation in the margin of the Revised Version of verse 33, and instead of reading, "he groaned in the spirit, and was troubled," we find, "he was moved with indignation in the spirit, and troubled himself." What was this indignation? We cannot think that it was caused by the unbelief of His friends, or even by the pretended sympathy of those malicious Jews who have hastened to accuse Him to the Pharisees, but we look further and deeper for the reason for this indignation.

Jesus now stood face to face with the last enemy, death. He saw what sin had done in destroying life and in corrupting the fair handiwork of God in the human body. He marked, also, the share that Satan had in all this, and His indignation was aroused; yes, His whole nature was stirred. Some read it, "He roused himself," instead of reading it as in our version, "He was troubled." Certainly, there would seem to be an active sense in the expression: it was not so much that He was troubled as that "He troubled himself." The waters of His soul were clear as crystal and therefore when troubled, they were not muddied; yet they were all stirred. It could be seen that His holy nature was in agitation, and an inarticulate expression of distress fell from Him. Between indignation at the powers of evil, grief for the family who had been bereaved by death, sorrow over those who stood by in unbelief, and a distressing realization of the effects of sin, the Lord's heart was evidently in a great storm. Instead of the thunder of threatening and the lightning of a curse, all that was perceptible of the inward tempest was a shower of tears, for "Jesus wept." A hurricane rushed through His spirit; all the forces of His soul were disturbed; He shuddered at the sight that was about to be set before Him; He was thrilled from head to foot with emotion; yet the result of the storm was not a word of terror or a glance of judgment but simply a blessed shower of tears: "Jesus wept." If all our righteous indignation displayed itself in tears of pity, we should have fulfilled the text, "Be ye angry, and sin not" (Eph. 4:26).

"Jesus wept." I have often been perturbed with the person who chopped up the New Testament into verses. He seems to have let the hatchet drop indiscriminately here and there. But I forgive him a great deal of blundering for his wisdom in letting these two words make a verse by themselves: "Jesus wept." This is a diamond of the first order, and it cannot have another gem set with it, for it is unique. Shortest of verses in words, but where is there a longer one in meaning? Add a word to the verse, and it would be out of place. No, let it stand in solitary sublimity and simplicity. You may even put a note of exclamation after it, and let it stand in capitals, "JESUS WEPT!" There is infinitely more in these two words than any sermonizer or student of the Word will ever be able to bring out of them even if he were to apply a microscope of the most attentive consideration. "Jesus wept." Instructive fact, simple but amazing, full of consolation, worthy of our sincere heed. Come, Holy Spirit, and help us to discover for ourselves the wealth of meaning contained in these two words!

We read of other men who wept. Abraham, when he buried Sarah, wept; Jacob had power with the angel, for he wept and prevailed; of David we are continually reading that he wept. His friend Jonathan and he once wept together and were not unmanly but were the more truly men for weeping. Of Hezekiah we read that he wept sore, and of Josiah that he poured forth tears over the sins of Judah. Jeremiah was a weeping prophet. I might continue the list, but if I did, it would not be at all remarkable that the sons of a fallen father should weep. With all the sin and sorrow that surrounds our manhood, it is no marvel that it should be said of any man, "He wept." The earth brings forth thorns and thistles, and the heart brings forth sorrow and sighing. Is there a man or woman who has not wept? Have we not all, sometimes, felt a sweet relief in tears? The marvel is that the sinless Son of God should, in the days of His flesh, know the meaning of strong crying and tears. The fact worthy to be noticed and recorded is that He wept.

Jesus Wept for He Is Truly Man

Many facts prove the completeness of our Lord's taking up of our humanity. Not in phantasm nor in fiction was Jesus a man, but in reality and truth He became one of us. He was born of a woman, wrapped in swaddling bands, fed from the breast. He grew as a child, was obedient to His parents, and increased in stature and in wisdom. In manhood He worked, He walked, He wearied. He ate as we do; we find it mentioned that He fasted and that He hungered. After His resurrection He ate a piece of broiled fish and a piece of a honeycomb to show that His body was real. His human nature was sustained, as ours is, by supplying it with food. Though on one occasion sustained by divine power, He fasted forty days and forty nights, yet as man He ordinarily needed food. He drank also and gave thanks both for food and for drink. We find Him sleeping with His head upon a pillow as well as resting by the well of Sychar. He suffered all the innocent infirmities of our nature. He was hungry and disappointed that he found no figs on the tree early one morning. In all things He was made like unto us: "Himself took our infirmities, and bare our sicknesses" (Matt. 8:17). His humanity was our humanity to the full, although without sin. Sin is not essential to humanity: it is a disease of nature; it is not a feature found in humanity as it came from the Creator's hand. The Man of men, in whom all true humanity is found in perfection, is Christ Jesus.

The fact that Jesus wept is a clear proof of this. *He wept, for He had human friendships.* Friendship is natural to man. Hardly is he a man who never had a friend to love. Men in going through the world make many acquaintances, but out of these they have few special objects of esteem whom they call friends. If they think to have many friends, they are probably misusing the name. All wise and good men have about them choice spirits with whom their fellowship is more free and in whom their trust is more confident than in all others. Jesus delighted to find rest in the quiet home at Bethany; and we read that "Jesus loved Martha, and her sister, and Lazarus" (John 11:5). Alas, every friendship opens a fresh door for grief, for friends are no more immortal than ourselves. "Jesus wept" at the grave of His friend just as you and I have done and must do again. Behold your Lord, like David weeping over Jonathan, and see how human He is in His friendships.

"Jesus wept" for *He was truly human in His sympathies.* He did not merely walk about among us and look like a man, but at a thousand points He came into contact with us. Jesus was always in touch with sorrow; happy are they who are in touch with *Him!* Our Lord saw Mary and Martha weeping and the Jews weeping who were with them, and He caught the contagion of their grief. His sympathies were with sorrowing ones, and for this reason, among others, He was Himself "a man of sorrows, and acquainted with grief" (Isa. 53:3). He loved first His Father in heaven, whose glory was His main object; but He loved intensely His chosen, and His sympathy with them knew no bounds. "In all their affliction he was afflicted" (Isa. 63:9). Jesus was far more tender toward humanity than any other man has ever been. He was the great Philanthropist.

Alas, man is often the cruelest foe of man. None more unkind to man than men. Not the elements of nature in their fury nor wild beasts in their rage nor diseases in their terror have made such havoc among men as men drunk with the war spirit. When has there been such cruel hatred on the part of the most savage monster toward man as has raged in the hearts of bloodthirsty warriors? To this hatred our Lord was a perfect stranger. There was no hardness in His heart. He was love, and only love; and through His love He descended into the depths of grief with the beloved ones whose lot was sorrowful; and He carried out to the full that sacred precept, "Weep with them that weep" (Rom. 12:15). Jesus was no unsuffering seraph, no cherub incapable of grief, but He was bone of our bone and flesh of our flesh; and therefore "Jesus wept."

Jesus was man for *He was stirred with human emotions.* Every emotion that ever thrilled through your bosom, so far as it is not sinful, has had its like in the bosom of the Lord Jesus Christ. Jesus could be angry, for we read that "he looked round about on them with anger" (Mark 3:5). He could be moved with compassion for a fainting crowd or with scorn toward a crafty ruler. Did He not speak with great indignation of the scribes and Pharisees? Yet, was He not tender as a nurse with a child when cheering the penitent? He would not break the bruised reed or quench the smoking flax, yet He uttered faithful warnings and made terrible exposures of hypocrisy. Our Savior, at the moment described in our text, felt indignation, pity, love, desire, and other emotions. He who is all tenderness was stirred from head to foot. He was troubled, and He troubled Himself. As when water is shaken in a glass bottle, so was His whole nature shaken with a mighty emotion as He stood at the grave of Lazarus, confronting death. Our Lord proved Himself a man when it was said that "Jesus wept."

Note, too, that *His pure body and His sinless soul were originally constituted as ours are.* When His body was formed according to that Scripture, "a body hast thou prepared me" (Heb. 10:5), that holy thing had in it the full apparatus of grief. Where there is no sin, one would say there should be no sorrow; but in the formation of that blessed body, all the arrangements for the expression of grief were as full prepared as in the case of anyone. His eyes were made to be fountains of tears, even as are ours. He had about His soul also all the capacity for mental grief. His heart was made capacious enough to be a reservoir wherein should be gathered up great floods of grief. See how the sorrow bursts forth in a great flood! Mark the record of that flood with those amazing words: "Jesus wept."

Beloved, have a clear faith in the humanity of Him whom you rightly worship as your Lord and your God. Holding His divinity without doubt, hold His manhood without mistake. Realize the actual manhood of Jesus in all lights. Three times we read He wept. Doubtless He sorrowed often when He was not seen, but three times He was known to weep. In this instance, it was the weeping of a friend over the grave of a friend. A little later on, after a day of triumph, our Lord beheld the city of Jerusalem and wept over it (Luke 19:41)—the weeping of a prophet concerning judgments that He foresaw. It is not recorded by any evangelist, but the writer of Hebrews tells us that with strong crying and tears, Jesus made appeal to Him who "was able to save him from death, and was heard in that he feared" (Heb. 5:7). This third record sets forth the weeping of our Substitute as a sacrifice before God. Treasure up in your mind these three memories: the weeping of the Friend in sympathy with bereavement, the weeping of the Judge lamenting the sentence that He must deliver, and the weeping of the Surety as He suffers for us, bearing griefs that were not His own or sins in which He had no part. Thus, three times was it true that "Jesus wept."

Jesus Was Not Ashamed of His Human Weakness

He could have repressed His tears—many men do so constantly. I do not doubt that there may be great sorrow, very great sorrow, where there is no open expression of it. In fact, most of you must have felt times when grief has struck you such a stunning blow that you could not weep, you could not recover yourself sufficiently to shed tears: the heart was all on fire with anguish, but the eyes refused the cooling drops. The Savior could doubtless, if so He wished, have hidden His grief; but He did not choose to do so, for He was never unnatural. As "the holy child Jesus," He was free from pride and wore His heart where men could see it.

For, first, remember *His talk when He spoke to His disciples.* He never concealed His poverty. There is an idea that respectability is maintained by the pretense of riches whereby real need is hidden. It is thought disreputable to seem to be poor, even when you are. But our Lord did not follow such a course, for He said, "Foxes have holes, and birds of the air have nests; but the Son of man hath not where to lay his head" (Luke 9:58). Though He was rich, yet for our sakes He became poor, and He was never ashamed to let it be known that He was poor.

So, too, He was "despised and rejected of men" (Isa. 53:3), and He did not pretend to be unaware of it. He did not try to make out that He was exceedingly popular and that nobody had a word to say against Him, but He acknowledged that they had called the Master of the house Beelzebub. He knew what they had called Him, and He was not ashamed of being made the butt of ridicule and the target of reproach. When they ascribed His miracles to the power of Satan, He met the charges with an overwhelming reply, but He was not ashamed that slander had befallen Him as well as poverty. As for His suffering and death, how frequently do we find Him talking to His disciples about it, till Peter would have stopped

Him if he could! He spoke of being betrayed into the hands of sinners and despitefully entreated and spat upon, and then of being "lifted up." He even dwelt upon the smallest items of His coming passion. He had no wish to deny the fate that He knew awaited Him. Why not die and say nothing about it if so it must be? Not so the Savior. He has become a man, and He is not ashamed of what must necessarily follow as a part of His humiliation. Being found in fashion as a man, He becomes obedient to all that is required of His manhood, and before all observers He takes His place in the ranks. "Jesus wept."

Jesus wept although it might have been misunderstood and misrepresented. Do you not think that the Jews who stood there would sneeringly say, "See, He weeps! The miracle worker weeps! He calls Himself the Son of God, and yet He stands weeping there like an ordinary man!" Here was opportunity for scorn at His manifest weakness and even for blasphemy at the evident token of it; but our Lord did not act upon policy: He allowed His true feelings to be seen. He did not, like the Stoic, claim respect for His manhood by holding Himself within Himself and refusing to let men see that He was of like feelings with them. No, "Jesus wept." Tears may not be thought manly, but they are natural to man, and Jesus will not be unnatural. The enemies may say what they please and even blaspheme both Him and His God, but He will not act a part in the hope of silencing them. He acts the truth only and weeps as His kind heart suggests. He thinks more of Mary and of Martha, and of the comfort His sympathy may yield them, than of the petty ribaldry of unbelievers that may forge an excuse for itself out of the loving weakness of His humanity.

"Jesus wept," and thereby *He revealed His love to Lazarus*, so that others saw it and cried, "Behold how he loved him!" (John 11:36). This is one proof that our Lord does not hesitate to declare His love to His people. His cheeks are wet with tears such as those that drop from our eyes, and by those tears, all knew what manner of love He had toward His chosen. Blessed be His name! Many a great man might be willing to befriend a poor man with money but not with tearful love; but here the blessed Master, in the midst of the assembled multitude, confesses dead and rotting Lazarus as His friend and seals the covenant of His love with tears.

"Jesus wept"; *He was not ashamed to acknowledge the affliction that sin caused to His holy soul* nor the gash that the sight of death made in His heart. He could not bear to see the grave and its corruption. May we never think of the sin and misery of our race without sorrow! I confess I can never go through this huge city of London without feeling unhappy. I never pass from end to end without feeling a black and dark cloud hanging like a pall over my spirit. How my heart breaks for you, O sinful city of London! Is it not so you? What do you feel as you confront sin, poverty, ungodliness, drunkenness, and vice in the streets? These may well go through a man's heart like sharp swords. How Jesus would have wept over my great city! He could not stand in front of a lone grave, about to look upon a single corpse, without weeping. He saw in that one death the representation of what sin has done on so enormous a scale that it is impossible to compute the devastation, and therefore He wept. What have you not done, O Sin! You have slain all these, O Death! What a field of blood has Satan made this earth! The Savior could not stand unmoved in the presence of the destroyer or approach the gate of death's palace without deep emotion. Of this He was by no means ashamed. Holy emotion is not a weakness. If at any time in the midst of the world's wickedness and celebration you weep, do not hide those tears! Let the thoughtless see that there is one, at least, who fears God and trembles when the Holy One is provoked.

"Jesus wept," *though He was about to work a wonderful miracle.* The glory of His Godhead did not make Him ashamed of His manhood. Singular thing, too, that He should weep just before the joy of raising the dead to life. He is God, for He is about to call Lazarus out of the grave; but He is man just as much as ever, and therefore He weeps. Our Lord was as much man when He raised the dead as when He worked in the carpenter's shop at Nazareth. He was not ashamed to show His real manhood while He proved Himself the resurrection and the life. This day in the glory of heaven He wears His scars to show that though God, He is not ashamed to be recognized as man. He makes this one of His glorious names: "I am he that liveth, and was dead; and, behold, I am alive for evermore" (Rev. 1:18), therein describing His connection with our manhood in life and in death. Beloved, "Jesus wept" to show that He did not disdain the feebleness of that nature that He had taken up, that He might redeem it to God.

Remember that our Lord Jesus exercised three years of ministry, and each year was marked by a resurrection. He began by raising the little daughter of Jairus, upon whose unmarred countenance death had hardly set his seal (Mark 5:42). Then He went on to raise the young man at the gates of Nain, who was being carried out to His burial, dead but not yet corrupt (Luke 7:11–15). And now He consummates His glory by raising this Lazarus, who had been dead four days already. Yet, when He came to this crowning marvel and thus displayed the perfection of His Godhead, He did not disdain to stand before all and weep. Jesus is the Resurrection and the Life, yet "Jesus wept."

Jesus Is Our Instructor in Weeping

Observe why Jesus wept and learn a lesson from it. He wept because *this was His method of prayer on this occasion.* A great miracle was to be worked, and great power was needed from on high. As man, the Lord Jesus cries to God with intense sincerity and finds the fittest embodiment for His prayer in weeping. No prayer will ever prevail with God more surely than a liquid petition that, being distilled from the heat, trickles from the eye and waters the cheek. Thus is God won when He hears the voice of your weeping. The angel at Peniel will slip from Jacob's dry hands but moisten them with tears, and Jacob will hold Him fast. Before the Lord Jesus puts forth the power that raises Lazarus from the grave, He appeals to God with strong crying and tears. The Father appears for His weeping Son; and you, dear friend, if you want to win in prayer, must weep in prayer. Let your soul arouse itself to eager desire, and trouble itself to anguish, and then you will prevail. "Jesus wept" to teach us how to baptize our prayers to God in a wave of heart grief.

"Jesus wept" because *before He would arouse the dead He would be Himself aroused.* A word of His could have worked the wonder; yes, His mere will would have been enough. But for our instruction He did not make it so. There was a kind of evil that went not out but with prayer and fasting, and here was a kind of death that would not yield unless the Savior groaned and wept. Without great exertion of the life of Jesus, the death in Lazarus could not be subdued. Therefore the Lord aroused Himself and stirred up all His strength, troubling all His being for the struggle on which He entered.

Learn that if you want to do any great good in saving sinners, you must not be half asleep yourself: you must be troubled even to tears. Perhaps the most difficult thing in winning souls is to get ourselves into a proper state. The dead may bury the dead, but they cannot raise the dead. Until a man's whole soul is moved, he will not move his fellow. He might possibly succeed with those who are willing to be impressed, but the careless will be unmoved by any man who is unmoved himself. Tears storm a passage for warnings. If Christ's whole self must be stirred before Lazarus is raised, we must be thrilled before we can win a soul.

The fingers of decay are unwinding a goodly fabric that once was worn by the soul of Lazarus, and no voice can effectually command them to pause but one that sounds forth from a bursting heart. That "stinking" of which Martha spoke can only be turned into the sweet odors of grateful life by the salt tears of infinite love. It is still more so in our case. We must feel, if others are to feel. Never go into the classroom or the place of outreach with only one eye open; this will never do. Your Lord was all alive and all sensitive, and you must be the same. How can you expect to see His power exercised on others if you do not feel His emotion in yourself? You must be quickened into tenderness as He was, or you will not receive His life-giving power. When I am weak, then am I strong. "Jesus wept" when He raised dead Lazarus.

Jesus wept *in full knowledge of several things that might have prevented His weeping.* You have sometimes thought to yourself when weeping at the grave of a loved one that you have been wrong in doing so, but this is not the case. Our Savior wept, though He knew that Lazarus was safe enough. I do not know what had happened to the soul of Lazarus. When Scripture is silent, it is not my place to speak. But wherever Lazarus was, he was perfectly safe, and still "Jesus wept." Moreover, Jesus knew that He was going to raise Lazarus to life. Sometimes we are told that if we really believed that our loved ones would rise again and that they are safe and happy even now, we could not weep. Why not? Jesus did. There cannot be any error in following where Jesus leads the way. Jesus knew, moreover, that the death of Lazarus was for the glory of God: He had said, "This sickness is not unto death, but for the glory of God" (John 11:4); and yet He wept! Tears that we may regard as wrong have now free admission into the realm of holiness. You may weep, for Jesus wept. He wept with full knowledge of the happiness of Lazarus, with full expectation of Lazarus' resurrection, and with the firm assurance that God was glorified even by Lazarus' death. We may not, therefore, condemn what Christ allows.

"Jesus wept," but He did not sin. There was not even a particle of evil in any one of the Redeemer's tears. Salt there may have been, but not fault. Beloved, we can weep without sin. It is not a sin to weep for those whom God has taken away from us, nor for those who are suffering. Jesus wept in His Father's presence, saying in His sorrow the first word, "Father." He said, "Father, I thank thee" (John 11:41). If you can weep in such a way that all the while you feel God to be your Father and can thank Him and know that you are in His presence, your weeping is not blameworthy but healthy. Let such floods flow on, for such did Jesus. When you cannot smile or weep except by forgetting God and His law, then you are offending; but if you can get up to your great Father's bosom and bury your head there, you may sob away without limit, for that which He permits is evidently no offense. Jesus wept, but He never murmured, never faulted God's ways, never rebelled. I think this is good instruction here. May the Holy Spirit teach it to us. May the Lord write it on every weeper's heart.

In This Is Jesus Our Comforter

To those who are of a heavy heart, "Jesus wept": *herein is our honor.* When you weep, you weep in good company, for Jesus wept. Let no man censure you lest they blame not only you but also Jesus.

"Jesus wept": *herein is our sonship vindicated.* Perhaps you have asked whether you can be a child of God and yet go on weeping. Was not Jesus the well-beloved Son, and yet He wept? What child did God ever have that did not weep? He had one Son without sin, but He never had a son without sorrow. He had a Son who never deserved a stroke of the rod, and yet against that Son the sword was awakened. For those who mourn, remember that Jesus is the Worthy Master of all mourners.

See now the real sympathy of Christ with His people, for *herein is comfort.* Jesus' sympathy lies not alone in words, not even wholly in deeds—it is more tender than these can be. Only His heart could express His tender sympathy, and then it was by tears—tears that were brought up like gold from the orebed of the heart, minted in the eyes, and then put in circulation as current coin of the merchant, each one bearing the King's image and superscription. Jesus is our fellow sufferer, and this should be our greatest solace. Oh, if we had a High Priest who knew not what it is to suffer as we do, it would be a most unhappy thing for us! If we fled to Him for refuge and found that He had known no grief and consequently could not understand us, it would be killing to a broken heart. If in my grief I fled to Jesus and there was about Him a secret inability to sympathize, an incapacity to admit me to His heart, I would dash myself against it and die in despair. A Jesus who never wept could never wipe away my tears. That were a grief I could not bear, if He could not have fellowship with me and could not understand my woe.

Then consider how bravely our Lord endured: *herein is confidence*. Tears did not drown the Savior's hope in God. Jesus lived. He triumphed notwithstanding all His sorrows; and because He lives, we shall live also. He says, "Be of good cheer; I have overcome the world" (John 16:33). Though our hero had to weep in the fight, yet He was not beaten. He came, He wept, He conquered. You and I share the tears of His eyes, and we shall share the diamonds of His crown. Wear the thorn crown here, and you shall wear the crown of glory hereafter.

Let this comfort you, too, that though He wept, He weeps no more: *herein is heaven begun below*. "Death hath no more dominion over him" (Rom. 6:9) in any sense or degree. Jesus had finished weeping. So shall it be with us before long. How I love that promise: "Neither shall there be any more pain" (Rev. 21:4)! Heaven is without a temple, for it is all devotion; and so is it without a hospital, for it is all health and love. It will come to us before long, for it has come to Jesus. "And God shall wipe away all tears from their eyes" (Rev. 21:4). We shall soon have no cause for sorrow and no possibility of grief, for as He is, so shall we be; and as He is perfectly blessed, we shall be blessed in Him.

In This Jesus Is Our Example

We should weep, for Jesus wept. *Jesus wept for others*. I do not know that He ever wept for Himself. His were sympathetic tears. He embodied the command, "Weep with them that weep" (Rom. 12:15). He has a narrow soul who can hold it all within the compass of his ribs. A true soul, a Christlike soul, lives in other men's souls and bodies as well as in its own. A perfectly Christlike soul finds all the world too narrow for its abode, for it lives and loves; it lives by loving, and loves because it lives. Think of other weepers and have pity upon the children of grief. Be touched in heart and moved to pity by the pains and the agonies of the many now lying in our hospitals and by the even greater miseries of those who suffer for lack of medicine and care because they cannot get to the hospitals. How must those suffer who have bad nursing and little food, and in the winter suffer with the cold. You and I may never suffer as they do, but at least let us grieve on their account and stand ready to help them to the best of our ability.

In another matter, our Lord is our example; learn from Him that *our indignation against evil will best show itself in compassion for sinners.* I hear you denouncing the sin of drunkenness. I am glad to hear you: you cannot say anything too hard or too heavy about that degrading vice. But I pray you, end your denunciation with weeping over the poor drunkard. I heard you speak on the behalf of moral purity, and you smote the monsters of lasciviousness with all your force. I wish more strength to your arm! But when you have finished, sit down and weep, that such filthiness should defile men and women who are your fellow creatures. A flood of tears before the Holy God will do far more than the hugest roll of petitions to our politicians. "Jesus wept," and His tears were mighty weapons against sin and death. You feel indignant of the lazy, idle, loafing vagabonds whose very illness is produced by their own vice: I cannot condemn your virtuous wrath. But if you should in all things imitate Jesus, please note that it is written not that Jesus thundered but that He wept. Let indignation have pity mixed with it. I do not like lightning without rain, nor indignation without tears. You will do more good to the offenders and more good to yourself and more good to the best of causes if pity moistens all. You may, if you will, beat the terrible drum and sound the war trumpet, but the noise will rather deafen than soften. The voice of your weeping will be heard deep down in the soul and work more wonders than thunders of denunciation.

Last, when you have wept, *imitate your Savior—do something!* If the chapter before us had finished with "Jesus wept, and went about His daily business," it would have been a poor one. If nothing had come of it but tears, it would have been a great falling off from the usual ways of our blessed Lord. A cup of tears by itself is not worth much to anyone. But Jesus wept and then commanded, "Take ye away the stone" (John 11:39). He cried, "Lazarus, come forth" (John 11:43)! When Lazarus struggled out of the tomb, Jesus said, "Loose him, and let him go" (vs. 44). Some of you are full of pity for the sick, but I hope we shall not end in mere sentiment. If you cannot raise the dead, give something toward rolling away the stone that shuts the poor out of the hospital. If you cannot restore them to health, at least do something toward removing their maladies. Do what you can to loose a person from his graveclothes.

*O*ur Lord's grief was so intense that it could not be restrained by the occasion. The occasion was one entirely by itself: a brief gleam of sunlight in a cloudy day, a glimpse of summer amid a cruel winter. His disciples had brought the colt and had placed Him on it, and He was riding to the city that was altogether moved at His coming. The multitudes were eager to praise Him with waving boughs and loud hosannas, while His disciples in the inner circle were exulting in songs of praise that almost emulated the angelic chorales of the night of His birth. "Glory to God in the highest, and on earth peace, good will toward men" (Luke 2:14) found its echo when the disciples said, "Blessed be the King that cometh in the name of the Lord: peace in heaven, and glory in the highest" (Luke 19:38). Yet amid the hosannas of the multitude, while the palm branches were yet in many hands, the Savior stopped to weep. On the very spot where David had gone centuries before weeping, the Son of David stayed awhile to look upon the city and pour out His lamentation. That must have been deep grief that ran counter to all the demands of the moment and violated all the decorum of the occasion, turning a festival into a mourning, a triumph into a lament.

Chapter Two

The Lamentations of Jesus

And when he was come near, he beheld the city, and wept over it
—Luke 19:41.

ON THREE OCCASIONS we are told that Jesus wept. The first was when our Lord was about to raise Lazarus from the dead (John 11). He saw the sorrow of the sisters, He meditated upon the fruit of sin in the death and corruption of the body, and He groaned in spirit, and it is written that "Jesus wept." This verse stands alone, the smallest and yet in some respects the greatest verse of the whole Bible. It shines as a diamond of the highest quality. It contains a world of healing balm condensed into a drop. Here we have much in little: a wealth of meaning in two words. The second recording of Jesus' tears is the case before us: at the sight of the beloved but rebellious city, Jesus wept. The third occasion is mentioned in the fifth chapter of Hebrews where we are told that the Savior "in the days of his flesh, when he had offered up prayers and supplications with strong crying and tears unto him that was able to save him from death, and was heard in that he feared" (vs. 7). That passage relates to the Gethsemane agony, in which a shower of bitter tears was mingled with the bloody sweat.

The strength of His love strove with the anguish of His soul and, in the process, forced forth the sacred waters of His eyes.

Thus our Savior wept in *sympathy with domestic sorrow* and sanctified the tears of the bereaved. We, too, may weep when loved ones lie dead, for Jesus wept. There need not be rebellion in our mourning, for Jesus fully consented to the divine will and yet wept. We may weep and be guiltless of unbelief as to their resurrection, for Jesus knew that Lazarus would rise again, and yet He wept. Our Lord, in weeping over Jerusalem, showed His *sympathy with national troubles*, His distress at the evils that awaited His countrymen. Men should not cease to be patriots when they become believers. Saints should bemoan the ills that come upon the guilty people among whom they are numbered, and do so all the more because they are saints. Our Lord's third weeping was induced by *the great burden of human guilt* that pressed upon Him. This shows us how we, too, should look upon the guilt of men and mourn over it before God. But yet in this special weeping, Jesus is alone, for there was something in the tears of Gethsemane to which we cannot reach—He who shed them was then beginning to suffer as our substitute, and in that case He must tread the winepress alone, and of the people there must be none with Him. Behold beneath the olive trees a solitary weeper, enduring grief that, blessed be His name, is now impossible to us, since He has taken away the transgression that called for it.

We now turn to this second instance of our Savior's weeping, and here we find when we look at the original word that it is not exactly expressed by the word used in our English version. We read, "He beheld the city, and wept over it." But the Greek word means a great deal more than tears, and includes sobbings and cries. Perhaps it may be best to read it: "He lamented over it." He suffered a deep inward anguish, and He expressed it by signs of woe and by words that showed how bitter was His grief. Our subject will be the lamentations of Jesus, the lamentations of Him who could more truly say than the weeping prophet Jeremiah, "Behold, and see if there be any sorrow like unto my sorrow, which is done unto me.... I am the man that hath seen affliction by the rod of his wrath.... Mine eye runneth down with rivers of water for the destruction of the daughter of my people" (Lam. 1:12; 3:1, 48). Jesus is here a king by general acclamation but king of grief by personal lamentation. He is the sovereign of sorrow, weeping while riding in triumph in the midst of His followers. Did He ever look more kingly than when He showed the tenderness of His heart toward His rebellious subjects? The city that had been the metropolis of the house of David never saw so truly royal a man before, for he is fittest to rule who is readiest to sympathize.

We shall first consider *our Lord's inward grief* and then *His verbal lamentation.* Oh, for the power of the Spirit to bless the meditation to the melting of all our hearts! O Lord, speak to the rock and bid the waters flow, or, if it please You better, strike it with Your rod and make it gush with waters: only in some way make us answer to the mourning of our Savior.

Our Lord's Inward Grief

Our Lord's grief was so intense that *it could not be restrained by the occasion.* The occasion was one entirely by itself: a brief gleam of sunlight in a cloudy day, a glimpse of summer amid a cruel winter. His disciples had brought the colt and had placed Him on it, and He was riding to the city that was altogether moved at His coming. The multitudes were eager to praise Him with waving boughs and loud hosannas, while His disciples in the inner circle were exulting in songs of praise that almost emulated the angelic chorales of the night of His birth. "Glory to God in the highest, and on earth peace, good will toward men" (Luke 2:14) found its echo when the disciples said, "Blessed be the King that cometh in the name of the Lord: peace in heaven, and glory in the highest" (Luke 19:38). Yet amid the hosannas of the multitude, while the palm branches were yet in many hands, the Savior stopped to weep. On the very spot where David had gone centuries before weeping, the Son of David stayed awhile to look upon the city and pour out His lamentation. That must have been deep grief that ran counter to all the demands of the moment and violated all the decorum of the occasion, turning a festival into a mourning, a triumph into a lament.

Ah, He knew the hollowness of all the praises that were ringing in His ears! He knew that those who shouted hosanna today would, before many suns had risen, cry, "Crucify him! Crucify him!" He knew that His joyous entrance into Jerusalem would be followed by a mournful procession out of it, when they would take Him to the cross that He might die. He saw amid all the adulation of the moment the small level of sincerity that was in it, and He accepted it. But He lamented the abundance of mere outward excitement that would disappear like the froth of the sea, and so He stood and wept. It was a great sorrow, surely, that turned such a day of hopefulness into a season of anguish. It strikes me that all that day the Savior fasted, and if so, it is singular that He should have purposely kept for Himself a fast while others on His account held a festival. The reason He did so, I think, is this: Mark says, "And now the eventide was come, he went out unto Bethany with the twelve. And on the morrow, when they were come from Bethany, he was hungry: And seeing a fig tree afar off having leaves, he came, if haply he might find any thing thereon" (Mark 11:11–13). Such hunger would not have come upon Him had it not been preceded by a fast the day before. See, then, your Lord surrounded, as it were, with billows of praise, in the midst of a tumultuous sea of exultation, Himself standing as a lone rock, unmoved by all the excitement around Him. Deep was the grief that could not be concealed or controlled on such a day, when the sincere congratulations of His disciples, the happy songs of children, and the loud hosannas of the multitude everywhere welcomed Him.

The greatness of His grief may be seen also by the fact that *it overwhelmed other very natural feelings* that might have been and perhaps were excited by the occasion. Our Lord stood on the brow of the hill where He could see Jerusalem before Him in all its beauty. What thoughts it awakened in Him! His memory was stronger and quicker than ours, for His mental powers were unimpaired by sin, and He could remember all the great and glorious things that had been spoken of Zion, the city of God. Yet, as He remembered them all, no joy came into His soul because of the victories of David or the pomp of Solomon; temple and tower had lost all charm for Him; "the joy of the earth" brought no joy to Him, but at the sight of the venerable city and its holy and beautiful house, He wept. Modern travelers who have any soul in them are always moved by the sublimity of the spectacle from the Mount of Olives. Dean Stanley wrote, "Nothing in Rome, Memphis, Thebes, Constantinople, or Athens can approach it in beauty or interest," and yet this present Jerusalem does not compare with our Savior's. Still the Lord says nothing about this city, "Beautiful for situation" (Ps. 48:2), except to lament over it. If He counts the towers thereof and marks well her bulwarks, it is only to bemoan their total overthrow. All the memories of the past did but swell the torrent of His anguish in the foresight of her doom.

Something of admiration may have entered the Savior's holy breast, for before Him stood His Father's house, of which He still thought so much that even though He knew it would be left desolate, He took pains to purge it once again of the buyers and sellers who polluted it (Luke 19:45–46). That temple was built of white marble; much of it, the roof especially, was covered with slabs of gold. It must have been one of the fairest objects that ever a human eye rested upon as it glittered in the sun before Him. But what were those great and costly stones? What were those curious carvings to Him? His heart was saying within itself, "There shall not be left one stone upon another, that shall not be thrown down" (Luke 21:6). His sadness at the foresight of the city's desolation mastered His natural feeling of admiration for its present glory. His sorrow found no alleviation either in the past or in the present of the city's history; the dreadful future threw a pall over all.

His sadness mastered, too, the sympathy that He usually felt for those who were about Him. He would not stop His disciples from rejoicing, though the Pharisees asked Him, but He Himself took no share in the joy. Usually He was the most sensitive of men to all who were around Him, sorrowing with their sorrow and joying in their joy. But on this occasion, they may wave their palms and cut down branches of trees and spread them in the way, and children may shout Hosanna, but He who was the center of it all did not enter into the feeling of the hour. They triumph, but He weeps.

More striking still is the fact that His grief for others prevented all apprehension of Himself. As He beheld that city, knowing that within a week He would die outside its gates, He might naturally have begun to feel the shadow of His sufferings, but no trace of such emotion is discoverable. You and I in such a case, with the certainty of a speedy and ignominious death before us, would have been heavy about it: but Jesus was not. In all that flood of tears there was not one for His own death; the tears were all for Jerusalem's doom, even as He said afterward, "Daughters of Jerusalem, weep not for me, but weep for yourselves, and for your children" (Luke 23:28). He grieves for others, not for Himself, yet it must have been a very intense emotion that thus swept away, as with a torrent, everything else, so that He had neither joy for joy nor sorrow for sorrow, but His whole strength of feeling was poured forth from one sluice and ran in one channel toward the devoted city that had rejected Him and was about to put Him to death.

This great sorrow of His reveals to us the nature of our Lord. How complex is the person of Christ! He foresaw that the city would be destroyed, and though He was divine, He wept. He knew every single event and detail of the dreadful tragedy and used words about it of special historical accuracy that brings out His prophetic character, and yet the eye so clear in seeing the future was almost blinded with tears. He speaks of Himself as willing and able to have averted this doom by gathering the guilty ones under His wing, and thus He intimates His Godhead. While His nature on the one side of it sees the certainty of the doom, the same nature from another side laments the dread necessity. I will not say that His Godhead foresaw and His manhood lamented, for so mysteriously is the manhood joined to the Godhead that it makes but one person, and it were better to assert that the entire nature of Christ lamented over Jerusalem.

I have never been able to believe in an impassive God, though many theologians lay it down as an axiom that God cannot suffer. It seems to me that He can do or endure anything He wills to do and endure, and I for one cannot see that there is any special glorifying of God in the notion that He is incapable in any direction whatever. We can only speak of Him after the manner of men, and after that manner He speaks of Himself, and therefore there is no wrong in so doing.

It brings the great Father nearer when we see Him lamenting the wanderings of His children and joying in their penitent return. What but sorrow can be meant by such expressions as these? "How shall I give thee up, Ephraim? how shall I deliver thee, Israel? how shall I make thee as Admah? how shall I set thee as Zeboim? mine heart is turned within me, my repentings are kindled together" (Hos. 11:8). "Hear, O heavens, and give ear, O earth: for the LORD hath spoken, I have nourished and brought up children, and they have rebelled against me. The ox knoweth his owner, and the ass his master's crib: but Israel doth not know, my people doth not consider" (Isa. 1:2–3). Are these the words of an unfeeling God? I believe it is the Christ, the entire Christ, who both foretells the doom of Jerusalem and laments it. Some have even been staggered at the statement that Jesus wept. Certain of the early Christians even went the length of striking the passage out of the gospel because they thought that weeping would dishonor their Lord. They should have had more reverence for the inspired word and truer knowledge of their Master and should never have wished to obliterate a record that reflects the highest honor upon man's Redeemer.

Our Lord's lament gives us an insight into the great tenderness of His character. He is so tender that He not only weeps while weeping is of any avail but also laments when lamentation must be fruitless. He reminds me of a judge who, having before been a friend, warning, persuading, pleading with the prisoner, at last has the unutterable pain of condemning him. He puts on the black cap and, with many a sigh and tear, pronounces sentence, feeling the dreadful nature of the occasion far more than the criminal at the bar. He is overcome with emotion while he declares that the condemned must be taken to the place from where he came and there die a felon's death. Oh, the tender heart of Christ, that when it comes to pronouncing the inevitable sentence, "Behold, your house is left unto you desolate" (Luke 13:35), He cannot utter the right- eous word without lamentation.

In this our Lord reveals the very heart of God. Did He not say, "He that hath seen me hath seen the Father" (John 14:9)? Here, then, you see the Father Himself, even He who said of old, "As I live, saith the Lord GOD, I have no pleasure in the death of the wicked; but that the wicked turn from his way and live" (Ezek. 33:11). The doom *must be* pronounced, for infinite justice demands it, but mercy laments what she was not permitted to prevent. Tears fall amid the thunders, and though the doom is sealed by obstinate impenitence, judgment is evidently strange work to the patient Judge. This anguish showed how dreadful was the sentence, for what could stir the Savior so if the doom of sinners is a small affair? If the doom of guilt is such a trifle as some dream, I cannot understand the tears. The whole nature of Christ is convulsed as He thinks first of Jerusalem plowed as a field and her children slaughtered till their blood runs in rivers, and next as He beholds the doom of the ungodly, who must be driven from His presence and from the glory of His power to be the awful witnesses of divine justice and of God's hatred of evil. Thus standing on the brow of Olivet, the weeping Son of man reveals to us the heart of God, slow to anger, of great mercy, waiting to be gracious, and slow in executing His wrath.

For a practical lesson, we may remark that *this weeping of the Savior should encourage men to trust Him.* Those who desire His salvation may approach Him without hesitation, for His tears prove His hearty desires for our good. When a man who is not given to sentimental tears is seen to weep, we are convinced of his sincerity. When a strong man is passionately convulsed from head to foot and pours out lamentations, you feel that he is in downright earnest, and if that sincerity is manifested on your behalf, you can commit yourself to him. O weeping sinner, fear not to come to a weeping Savior! If you will not come to Jesus, it grieves Him; that you have not come long ago has wrung His heart; that you are still away from Him is His daily sorrow. Come, then, to Him without delay. Let His tears banish your fears; yes, He gives you better encouragement than tears, for He has shed drops for sinners not from His eyes alone but from His heart. He died that sinners who believe in Him might live. His whole body was covered with bloody sweat when He agonized for you. How can you doubt His readiness to receive you? The five scars that still remain upon His blessed person up there at the Father's right hand all invite you to approach Him. How shall He who wept and bled and died for sinners repulse a sinner who comes to Him at His bidding? Oh, come, come, come, I pray you, even now, to the weeping Sinner's Friend!

This, too, I think is *an admonishment to Christian workers.* Some of us came to Christ many years ago, and we now occupy ourselves with endeavoring to bring others to Him. In this blessed work, our Lord instructs us by His example. If we would have others come to Jesus, we must be like Jesus in tenderness; we must be meek, lowly, gentle, and sympathetic, and we must be moved to deep emotion at the thought that any should perish. Never let us speak of the doom of unbelievers harshly, flippantly, or without holy grief. The loss of heaven and the endurance of hell must always be themes for tears. That men should live without Christ is grief enough, but that they should die without Christ is an overwhelming horror that should grind our hearts to powder before God and make us fall on our faces and cry out to God for mercy and grace toward them. The deepest tenderness, it may be, some of us have yet to learn. Perhaps we are passing through a school in which we shall be taught it, and if we do but learn it, we need not care how severe the instructive discipline may need to be. We should not look on our cities without tears, nor even upon a single sinner without sorrow. We must preach tenderly and teach tenderly if we would win souls. We are not to weep continually, for even Jesus did not do that, yet we are always to feel a tender love toward men so that we should be ready to die for them if we might but save them from the wrath to come and bring them into the haven of the Savior's rest.

Let me add that I think the lament of Jesus should *instruct all those who would now come to Him as to the manner of their approach*. We should come to Jesus with sorrow and with prayer, even as it is written, "They shall come with weeping, and with supplications will I lead them" (Jer. 31:9). As Jesus meets you, you should meet Him. He shows you in what fashion to return, in what array to draw near, to your Redeemer, for He comes to you clothed in no robes but those of mourning, adorned with no jewels but the pearls of tears. Come to Him in the garments of humiliation, mourning for your sin. "Blessed are they that mourn: for they shall be comforted" (Matt. 5:4). Penitential sorrow works life in men. Only come to Jesus and tell Him you have sinned and are ashamed and desire to cease to do evil and to learn to do good. Come in all your misery and sorrow to the Man of sorrows who is even now on the road to meet you. He has said, "Him that cometh to me I will in no wise cast out" (John 6:37), and He will never change His word.

Our Lord's Verbal Lamentations

"If thou hadst known, even thou, at least in this thy day, the things which belong unto thy peace! but now they are hid from thine eyes" (Luke 19:42).

First, notice, He laments over *the fault by which they perished*: "If thou hadst known." Ignorance, willful ignorance, was their ruin. They did not know what they might have known, what they should have known, for they did not know their God. They knew not God; they knew not His only Son; they knew not Him who came in mercy to them with nothing but love upon His lips. This is the pity, that light is come into the world and men will not have it but love darkness rather than light. There are none so deaf as those who will not hear and none so blind as those who will not see. Yet there are such in all Christian congregations to whom God says, "O that thou hadst hearkened to my commandments! then had thy peace been as a river, and thy righteousness as the waves of the sea" (Isa. 48:18). Our Lord lamented over the inhabitants of Jerusalem, for they would have none of His counsel, they despised His reproof, and they did not choose the fear of the Lord. Willful ignorance led to obstinate unbelief; they chose to die in the dark rather than accept the light of the Son of God.

The Lord laments *the bliss that they had lost*, the peace that could not be theirs. "The things which belong to thy peace!" The name of Jerusalem signifies a vision of peace. But, alas, Jerusalem had lost its *salem*, or peace, and become a vision only, because she did not know and would not know her God. Oh, the joys they might have had! The delights of pardoned sin, the bliss of conscious safety, the joy of fellowship with God and His Son Jesus, the heavenly expectation of infinite glory, all might have been theirs, but they had put them away. "Oh that my people had hearkened unto me, and Israel had walked in my ways! I should soon have subdued their enemies, and turned my hand against their adversaries" (Ps. 81:13–14). God desires by His Spirit to reveal brighter things than our eyes have seen and sweeter joys than our ears have heard, and when we are willing and obedient, we will eat the fat of the land of His promise. We are awful losers if we are not reconciled to God and worse losers yet if we allow a false peace to beguile and fascinate us, leaving us on the arid sands of despair to seek for rest but find none. Soon shall a terrible sound be heard of the approaching vengeance of God, and there shall be no place of refuge for us.

When the Lord thought of what they had lost, He cried, "If thou hadst known." I feel ashamed to repeat His words because I cannot repeat them in the tone He used. Oh, to hear Jesus say these words! I think it might melt a heart of stone! But no. I am mistaken; even that would not do it, for those who did hear Him were not melted or reclaimed but went on their way to their doom as they had before. How hardened are the men who can trample on a Redeemer's tears! What wonder that they find a hell where not a drop of water can ever cool their parched tongues, tormented in the flame! If men are resolved to be damned, it is evident that the tears of the best, the most perfect of men cannot stop them. Woe is me! This is deeper cause for tears than all else besides, that men should be so desperately set on mischief that nothing but omnipotence will stop them from eternal suicide!

But our Lord also lamented over *the persons who had lost peace*. Observe that He says, "If thou hadst know, *even thou.*" Jerusalem was the favored city. It is one thing that Egypt did not know, or that

Tyre and Sidon did not know, but that Jerusalem should not know! Ah, if Jesus were standing in front of us now, He might weep over some of us as well. Some of us have grown up in a loving church where godly men and women cared for us. Some of us have listened to the exhortations of our father and had a mother who prayed and pleaded for us. Yet we have not entered the kingdom. Perhaps we have come right up to the edge of the borderland, but have not crossed the line of decision for Christ. There may be a thousand things that are hopeful about you, but there is one thing that damps your hope, causing you to procrastinate and not use your present opportunity. Jesus bids you that today is God's accepted time; postpone no longer the hour of decision. God have mercy on the sons and daughters of Christian parents who will not come to Him! You who have been enriched with Christian privileges, why will you die? It makes the Savior weep that you, even you, should refuse to know the things that make for your peace.

Our Lord wept because of *the opportunity that they had neglected.* He said, "At least in this thy day." It was such a favored day. In previous times, they had been warned by holy men, but now they had the Son of God Himself to preach to them. It was a day of miracles of mercy, a day of the unveiling of gospel grace, and yet they would not have Christ, though He had come so near to them and it was a day of merciful visitation such as other nations had not known. Perhaps today is such a day of visitation for you. Perhaps you feel some tender touch of the Spirit's power. Do not resist Him and cause this day also to pass away unimproved. The autumn comes to an end, and winter makes it approach. Shall these days in which the Spirit visits men depart while God shall declare that it does not become the dignity of His Spirit to always strive with flesh, and therefore He shall cease His operations and leave men to their own devices. I pray you to consider that Christ is weeping because revival days are being wasted by you. Do not in these best of days commit the worst of sins by still refusing to receive the gospel of God.

The Lord Jesus mourned again because *He saw the blindness that had stolen over them.* They had shut their eyes so tight that now they could not see. Their ears that they had shut had become dull and heavy, and their hearts were hardened. So they could not see with their eyes nor hear with their ears nor feel in their hearts nor be converted that He should heal them. Why, the truth was as plain as the sun in the heavens, and yet they could not see it; and so is the gospel to many. There is nothing plainer than the plan of salvation by looking to Jesus, and yet many have gone on so long resisting the sweetness and light of the Spirit of God that they cannot now see the Lord Jesus who is as the sun in the heavens. The kindest friends put the gospel before them in a way that has enlightened others but has not affected them. Christ groans because the things that belonged to the peace of Jerusalem were hid from their eyes as a punishment for refusing to see.

Finally, we know that the great floodgates of Christ's grief were pulled up because of *the ruin that He foresaw*. It is worth any man's time to read the story of the destruction of Jerusalem as it is told by the Jewish historian Josephus. It is one of the most harrowing of all records written by a human hand. It remains the tragedy of tragedies, and there never was and there never will be anything comparable to it. The people died of famine and pestilence and fell by thousands beneath the swords of their own countrymen. Women devoured the flesh of their own children, and men raged against each other with the fury of beasts. All ills seemed to meet in that doomed city, which was filled with horrors and surrounded by terrors. There was no escape; neither would the frenzied people accept mercy from the Romans. The city itself was the banqueting hall of death. Josephus says:

> All hope of escaping was now cut off from the Jews, together with their liberty of going out of the city. Then did the famine widen its progress and devour the people by whole houses and families. The upper rooms were full of women and infants that were dying by famine, and the lanes of the city were full of the dead bodies of the aged. The children, also, and the young men wandered about the market places like shadows, all swelled with the famine, and fell down dead wheresoever their misery seized them. For a time the dead were buried; but afterward, when they could not do that, they had them cast down from the wall into the valleys beneath. When Titus, on going his rounds along these valleys, saw them full of dead bodies, he gave a groan, and spreading out his hands to heaven, called God to witness this was not his doing.

While there is nothing in history to exceed this horror, this is nothing compared with the destruction of a soul. A man might look with complacency upon a dying body if he knew that within it was a soul that would live eternally in bliss and cause the body to rise again to equal joy. But for a soul to die is a catastrophe so terrible that the heavens might be clothed with sackcloth for its funeral. There is a death that never ends, the separation of the soul from God, which is the completest of all deaths. The separation of the soul from the body is but, as it were, a prelude and type of the far more dreadful death, the separation of the soul from God. Banished from hope, existing but not living, and that forever. What a condition must this be! I shall draw no picture: words fail, but what of the meaning of the Savior's words: "These shall go away into everlasting punishment"(Matt. 25:46)? If we know anyone to whom this doom will happen, we might make a ring around them and lead them home, rending our garments and tearing our hair, for it would be a far greater grief than if we knew that they would die by the sword or famine.

Do you hear our Savior's grief expressed in other words He spoke? "O Jerusalem, Jerusalem, thou that killest the prophets, and stonest them which are sent unto thee, how often would I have gathered thy children together, even as a hen gathereth her chickens under her wings, and ye would not!" (Matt. 23:37). Do you see His grace and grief? These people killed the prophets, and yet the Lord of prophets would have gathered them. His love had gone so far that even prophet killers He would have gathered. Is it not wonderful that there should be grace enough in Christ to gather adulterers, liars and thieves and to forgive and change them; and yet they will not be gathered? This is a grief of love. If it had been a fact that Christ would not, then I cannot understand His tears. But when He says, "I would, but ye would not," then I see the deep reason for His anguish.

And finally we hear as He foretells their fate: "Behold, your house is left unto you desolate" (Matt. 23:38). Note the contrast in the two words *gathered* and *desolate*. *Gathered* is such a beautiful picture. You see the little chicks fleeing from danger when they hear the cluck of the mother hen; they gather together, and they come under her wings. Did you ever hear that little, pretty cry they make when they are all together with their heads buried in the feathers? How warm and comfortable they are! This is where Jesus would gather us, under the warm breast of the eternal God, feeling His love with the rest of the people, joying and rejoicing in a communion of complete security. But when one will not be gathered in, he is left *desolate*, without a friend or helper. You will call them to the saints, but they shall not be able to help you. Each cherub waves his fiery sword to keep you from the gate of Paradise. There is no help for you in God when once you die without Him, no help for you anywhere. Desolate! For good reason the tender Savior weeps over men, since they will perversely choose such a doom.

The day hastens on when Christ will come a second time, and then He shall behold a new Jerusalem, a spiritual Jerusalem, built by divine hands. The foundations are of jewels and the gates are of pearl. How He will rejoice over it! He shall rest in His love, He shall rejoice over it with singing. He will shed no tear then, but He will see in the Jerusalem from above the travail of His soul, and He shall be satisfied. When Zion shall be built up, the Lord shall appear in His glory, and the marriage of the Lamb will have come. Who would not come to Jesus?

Further, let us see how like the Son of God was to us in His intensity of prayer. I wish I knew how to write upon a theme so sacred. One needs to put off his shoes from his feet upon this doubly consecrated ground. The intensity of His prayer was such that our Lord expressed Himself "with strong crying and tears." The evangelists do not record His tears, but the Holy Spirit here reveals what human eyes could not have seen. He pleaded with God until His pent-up grief demanded audible utterance, and He began to cry. He said, so that the disciples heard Him a stone's cast away, "My Father, if it be possible, let this cup pass from me." His voice grew louder as the stream of His sorrows forced a channel for itself. There was great strength in His cries—they were "strong crying"; they were deep, plaintive, touching, heartbreaking: "If it be possible!" We may be thankful that we did not hear the cries of that sore distress that fell upon our great Substitute. Cries are weak things, but His were strong crying—strong with the heart of the Great Father. When He ceased His crying and was silent, His tears took up the strain. The Lord heard a voice in His tears, and who shall say which spoke more loudly, His crying or His tears?

Chapter Three

Our Sympathizing High Priest

Who in the days of his flesh, when he had offered up prayers and supplications with strong crying and tears unto him that was able to save him from death, and was heard in that he feared; Though he were a Son, yet learned he obedience by the things which he suffered; And being made perfect, he became the author of eternal salvation unto all them that obey him; Called of God an high priest after the order of Melchisedec—Hebrews 5:7–10.

THE HOLY SPIRIT REMINDS US in Hebrews 5 that two things were necessary in a high priest: first, he must be suitable for the men for whom he stood, and next, he must be acceptable with God. "For every high priest taken from among men is ordained for men in things pertaining to God" (5:1). He must be fit from both points of view, both manward and Godward. Our Lord Jesus Christ was ordained of God from of old and did not of Himself assume the position of high priest. The prophets spoke of Him as the Messiah of God, and Jehovah Himself declared, "Thou art a priest for ever, after the order of Melchisedec" (5:6). When He came into the world, the Holy Spirit bore witness to His being the Son of the Highest. At His baptism there came a voice from heaven saying, "This is my beloved Son, in whom I am well pleased" (Matt. 3:17), and that same voice was three times heard declaring the same fact. The Father has given further testimony to the mission of Christ, "in that he hath raised up Jesus again" (Acts 13:33), and has caused Him to enter into the heavenly places on our behalf. Moreover, He has given Him a pledge that as Melchizedek, being both king and priest, He shall sit at His right hand until He has made His enemies His footstool. Our Lord Jesus has been chosen, ordained, and glorified as our "great high priest, that is passed into the heavens" (Heb. 4:14). This is the groundwork for our comfort in our Lord Jesus, for we know that He is one with the Father and that all things are done by Him as the messenger of the covenant, the authorized representative of Jehovah our God.

It is clear that *our Lord Jesus is preeminently suited to be a High Priest for us, viewed from the humanity side.* A high priest must be one who can have compassion on the ignorant and weak. He must be one who has learned compassion in the school of suffering so that he can comfort the afflicted. There is no learning sympathy except by suffering. It cannot be studied from a book; it must be written on the heart. You must go through the fire if you would have sympathy with others who tread the glowing coals; you must bear your own cross if you would feel for those whose life is a burden to them. We live in a world of sin and sorrow, and we ourselves are sinful and sorrowful; we need one who can put away our sin and become a sharer in our sorrow. If he cannot go with us through all the rough places of our pilgrim way, how can he be our guide? If he has never traveled in the night himself, how can he whisper consolation to us in our darkest hours? We have a fully qualified High Priest in our Lord Jesus Christ who is perfect in this capacity.

The great suitability of Christ for His work will be seen as we view Him in three aspects. I will first consider Him as *a supplicant,* then view Him as *a Son,* and finally regard Him as *a Savior.* Come, Holy Spirit, and take the things of Christ and show them to us.

Christ as a Supplicant

The text begins with a word that reveals *Christ's weakness:* "Who in the days of his flesh." Our Lord was in such a condition that He pleaded out of weakness with the God who was able to save. Living with the weakness of the flesh, Jesus was often in prayer. While the occasions recorded in Scripture are many, these are no doubt merely a few examples of a far greater number. Jesus was constantly in prayer; He was praying even when His lips did not utter a sound. His heart was always in communion with the Great Father above. This is said to have been the case "in the days of his flesh." This term is used to distinguish His life on earth from His former place in glory. From of old the Son of God dwelt with the Father, but He was not then a partaker of human nature, and the eternal ages were not "the days of his flesh." Then He could not have entered into that intimate sympathy with us that He now exercises since He has been born at Bethlehem and has died at Calvary. His mortal life was days of His weakness, humiliation, labor, and suffering. It is true that He wears our nature in heaven, for He said to His disciples after His resurrection, "Handle me, and see; for a spirit hath not flesh and bones, as ye see me have" (Luke 24:39). But yet we should not call the period of His exaltation at the right hand of the Father "the days of his flesh." He prays still: in fact, He continually makes intercession for the transgressors, but it is in another style from how He prayed while He was on earth.

During the days of His life on earth there were some that peculiarly deserved to be called "the days of His flesh"—days in which His humanity pushed itself to the front. Then men saw less of His greatness as a teacher and more of His suffering as a man. One such day was when He went to Gethsemane and was "exceeding sorrowful, even unto death" (Matt. 26:38). He was very heavy, because the shadow of His cross fell upon Him with a denser darkness as He drew nearer to His death upon it. When the dread desertion by God that was the center of His grief began to startle Him, when men esteemed Him "stricken, smitten of God, and afflicted" (Isa. 53:4), then were "the days of his flesh." Prostrate under the olive trees, pouring out His inmost soul in plaintive entreaties, even to a bloody sweat, your Lord is a supplicant in weakness of the flesh.

Consider the Lord's pleading "in the days of his flesh" as a matter of fact. Do not dream of Him as though He were a phantom and of His prayers as if they were part of a mere show. He was a real man, and His prayers were as real as yours can be. Believe in Jesus as man. You would be upset with anyone who would diminish the glory of His Godhead, so do not yourself take away from Him the truth of His humanity. He was in very deed made flesh and dwelt among us. This was the case even when His apostles beheld His glory, "the glory as of the only begotten of the Father, full of grace and truth" (John 1:14). We must get a firm grip of the true humanity or else we lose the sacrificial death, the resurrection, and all the rest; and the brotherhood of our Lord, which is a grand source of consolation, also disappears. Remember that He who sits at the right hand of God was once here in the likeness of sinful flesh. He who shall shortly come to judge the quick and the dead passed through a period of limitation, suffering weariness, since He was in human flesh. He knew poverty, sickness, reproach, and temptation. Inasmuch as He has passed through such days as these, He is able to be the High Priest of believers, who also are passing through the days of their flesh. We know too well that we are partakers of flesh and blood, and it is no small comfort that our Lord took part of the same.

In the days of His flesh our divine Lord felt *His necessities*. The words, "he offered up prayers and supplications," prove that He had many needs. Men do not pray and plead unless they have greater need than this world can satisfy. Men work for what they can get by working and pray for that which can by no other means be obtained. The Savior offered no petitions by way of mere form; His supplications arose out of an urgent sense of His need of heavenly aid. It is difficult to realize it, but so it is, that our divine and innocent Savior placed Himself in such a condition for our sakes that His needs were manifold. Of course, as God He could come under no necessity; but being man, like ourselves, He did not permit the power of His Godhead to destroy the manlike weakness of the flesh. Hence, He endured such necessities as we do and resorted, as we must, to the one all-sufficient source of supply, approaching His Father by prayer. He sought for blessings with prayers; He pleaded against evil with supplications. His approaches to God were many—"prayers and supplications"—and they were manifold in their character, for He presented prayers of all kinds. Especially in the garden, He cried again and again, "If it be possible, let this cup pass from me" (Matt. 26:39). Yes, our Savior really did pray. When you, in your heaviness, shut the door of your room and kneel in prayer, when that prayer gathers strength and you fall flat upon your face in agony, when you cry and weep before the Most High under a sinking sense of need, it is hard for you to think that Jesus ever did the same. But He did so. He asked as really as you ask; He implored and sought, He entreated and wrestled, even as you must do. He knows that solitary place on Carmel, where Elijah bowed his head between his knees and cried seven times unto the Lord. He knows the turning of the face to the wall and the weeping of the sorrowful eyes, even as Hezekiah knew them. He can have pity upon you in your loneliness, your distraction, your apparent desertion, your sinking of heart, your sorrowfulness even unto death. Look to Him, then, in your night of weeping and be of good cheer.

Those of you who are only now beginning to pray, I would encourage you to remember Jesus as setting you the example of praying. If your prayers have but few words in them and are mainly made up of crying and tears, yet in this they are like those of your Savior, and so you may hope that they will be accepted. If you are afraid that your prayers are shut out of heaven, remember how the Savior complains in the twenty-second psalm, "O my God, I cry in the daytime, but thou hearest not; and in the night season, and am not silent" (vs. 2). He was heard in the end, but at the beginning He seemed to plead in vain. Jesus prayed under discouragements: what He did Himself, He will help you to do. He knows what the agony of prayer means, and He will cast a brother's eye on you when in the bitterness of your repentance you seek the Lord. How clear it is that we have a suitable High Priest of tender heart and loving soul!

Further, let us see how like the Son of God was to us in *His intensity* of prayer. I wish I knew how to write upon a theme so sacred. One needs to put off his shoes from his feet upon this doubly consecrated ground. The intensity of His prayer was such that our Lord expressed Himself "with strong crying and tears." The evangelists do not record His tears, but the Holy Spirit here reveals what human eyes could not have seen. He pleaded with God until His pent-up grief demanded audible utterance, and He began to cry. He said, so that the disciples heard Him a stone's cast away, "My Father, if it be possible, let this cup pass from me." His voice grew louder as the stream of His sorrows forced a channel for itself. There was great strength in His cries—they were "strong crying"; they were deep, plaintive, touching, heartbreaking: "If it be possible!" We may be thankful that we did not hear the cries of that sore distress that fell upon our great Substitute. Cries are weak things, but His were *strong* crying—strong with the heart of the Great Father. When He ceased His crying and was silent, His tears took up the strain. The Lord heard a voice in His tears, and who shall say which spoke more loudly, His crying or His tears?

When a man so courageous, so patient as Jesus, takes to cries and tears, we may be sure that the sorrow of His heart has passed all bounds. His soul within Him must have been bursting with grief. We know it was so by another sign, for the lifeblood forgot to course in its usual channels and overflowed its banks in a sweat of blood. I do not think, as some do, that it was merely a sweat such as is common to labor, but I believe it was a sweat of blood, or the expression would not have been used, "as it were great drops of blood falling down to the ground" (Luke 22:44). A sweat of blood has now and then been seen upon men in great and fatal alarm, but the Savior's was more wonderful than any of these cases, for so profuse was this bloody sweat that it was as it were great drops. This was prayer indeed, supplication that exhausted His whole manhood. Body, soul, and spirit were now upon the rack of anguish and upon the strain of agony. Jesus pleaded with God after a more piteous, painful, terrible, and powerful sort than you and I have yet attained. But here is the point: if you find yourself in a dark, dark hour and feel that the heavens are brass to your prayers, remember Jesus in the days of His flesh. Usually it may be you are very quiet and perhaps wordless in prayer, but now you cannot refrain yourself. As Joseph cried so that the Egyptians in the house of Pharaoh heard him, so do you give vent to your agony. Be not ashamed of your weakness, your Lord did so before you. Strong as you are, you weep like a child. Do not apologize lest you seem to accuse your Savior. Behold, you are not alone! Jesus is passing through the deeps with you. See the bloodstained footprint of your Lord. Your utmost anguish is known to Him. Fear not. Commit your way to the Lord, even in this worst part of it. Trust Him when the iron enters into your soul. Leave all in His experienced hands.

If you have never trusted the Lord, are you not attracted to Him? If He suffered all this, can He not meet our case? By all this He was made perfect as a High Priest; oh, can you not trust Him? Is He not able to enter into your misery? Oh, darkened hearts, is there not light here for you? When you pray with anguish, Jesus perfectly understands the situation. Oh, you that loathe yourselves, you daughters of melancholy and children of despair, can you not see in the marred visage of your Redeemer a reason for trusting Him? Since from His lips you hear strong crying, and from His eyes you see showers of tears, you may well feel that His is a sympathetic spirit to whom you may run in the hour of danger, even as the chicks seek the wings of the hen.

Still, to proceed with the text, we have seen our Lord's needs and the intensity of His prayer. Now note *His understanding* in prayer. He prayed "unto him that was able to save him from death." The expression is startling; the Savior prayed to be saved. In His direst woe He prayed thoughtfully and with a clear apprehension of the character of Him to whom He prayed. It is a great help in devotion to pray intelligently, knowing well the character of God to whom you are speaking. Jesus was about to die, and therefore the aspect under which He viewed the great Father was "him that was able to save him from death." This passage may be read in two ways: it may mean that He would be saved from actually dying if it could be done consistently with the glorifying of the Father, or it may mean that He pleaded to be saved out of death, though He actually descended into it. The word may be rendered either *from* or *out of*. The Savior viewed the great Father as able to preserve Him in death from the power of death, so that He should triumph on the cross, and also as able to bring Him up again from among the dead. Remember how He said in Psalm 16: "For thou wilt not leave my soul in hell; neither wilt thou suffer thine Holy One to see corruption" (vs. 10). Jesus had faith in God concerning death and prayed according to that faith. This brings our blessed Lord very near to us; He prayed in faith even as we do. He believed in the power of God to save Him from death, and even when cast down with fear, He did not let go His hold on God. He pleaded just as you and I should plead, impelled by fear and encouraged by faith. He has condescended to set us an example that we may copy. He has come into living companionship with us in our most urgent supplications. Therefore, trust in Him.

It will further help you if I now call your attention to *His fear:* "And was heard in that he feared." That is to say, Jesus had a fear, a natural and not a sinful fear, and from this fear He was delivered by the strength brought to Him from heaven by the angel. God has implanted in all of us the love of life, and we cannot part from it without a pang: our Lord felt a natural dread of death. If it is said that the Savior was too courageous to know the fear of death, I beg to remark that He was the more courageous because He so calmly encountered that which He feared. Martyrs have died without the preceding dread that fell upon our Lord; but remember that the help of God that sustained *them* was taken away from Jesus. Consider, also, that His death differed from that of all others of our race, for in His death there was condensed the penalty due to sin. To the righteous man, death is not now a penalty but a mode of going home. To Jesus, it was in the fullest sense the penalty of death for human guilt. He saw before Him, as we do not, all the pains and torments of death. He knew what He had to bear and fore-tasted in the garden of Gethsemane the pain involved in being a surety for sinful man. The vials of God's wrath were about to be poured upon Him, and Jehovah was heard saying, "Awake, O sword, against my shepherd, and against the man that is my fellow, saith the LORD of hosts" (Zech. 13:7). Jesus saw the abyss into which He must fall. If no dread had come upon Him, I think the very essence of the atoning suffering would have been absent. Fear must take hold of Him—not that of a coward but that of one terribly oppressed. His soul was "exceeding sorrowful, even unto death."

So when you tremble after sipping your cup of bitterness, think of Jesus trembling, too. When you enter into the valley of the shadow of death and feel yourself greatly disturbed at the prospect before you, think of Jesus who was heard in His fear. Come, you that fear, and find help in One who also feared. Borrow courage from One who out of fear prayed Himself into victory. Think of Him who cried to God, "But be not thou far from me, O LORD: O my strength, haste thee to help me" (Ps. 22:19). Trust your soul with Him who in the days of His flesh cried out in anguish, "My God, my God, why hast thou forsaken me?" (Matt. 27:46).

But then notice another thing in the text, namely, *His success* in prayer, which also brings Him near to us. He was heard "in that he feared." O my soul, to think that it should be said of my Lord that He was heard, even as I am heard. Yet the cup did not pass from Him; neither was the bitterness thereof in the least lessened. When we are compelled to bear our thorn in the flesh and receive no other answer than "my grace is sufficient for thee" (2 Cor. 12:9), let us see our fellowship with Jesus and Jesus' fellowship with us. Jesus came forth from His agony saying, "Thou hast heard me from the horns of the unicorns. I will declare thy name unto my brethren: in the midst of the congregation will I praise thee" (Ps. 22:21–22). Oh, what a brother Christ is, since He, too, cried and wept and had power with God and prevailed! When God has sent from above and drawn us out of many waters, the Lord Jesus, the constant companion of all our experiences, is there to sing with us and rejoice with us. Can we not trust Him? If Jesus rises with us to the highest note of the scale and if He also comes down with us to the deepest bass that the human voice can reach, then we may con-clude that all along He is in unison with us in all the intervening notes. Let us today feel that Jesus is like ourselves in all but our sin and that we may fearlessly come and trust Him as we would trust a father or a brother or as a fond wife confides in her husband of her love.

Jesus as a Son

The Sonship of our dear Savior is well attested. The Lord declared this in Psalm 2: "Thou art my Son; this day have I begotten thee" (vs. 7). Three times did the voice out of the excellent glory proclaim this truth, and He was "declared to be the Son of God with power, according to the spirit of holiness, by the resurrection from the dead" (Rom. 1:4). Yes, He who cried, He who wept, He who pleaded until He came to a bloody sweat, and He from whom the cup could not pass till He had drained it to the dregs, was nevertheless the only begotten of God. So when you are put to great grief, do not doubt your sonship. What son is there whom the father does not discipline? When you are in heaviness through manifold trials, do not listen to the insinuations of the enemy: "If you are a son of God." Even if you should have to ask "Why have You forsaken me?" do not doubt your sonship. Your faith should be founded not upon your own enjoyments but upon the promise and the faithfulness of God. You are as much a son when you walk in the dark as when you rejoice in the light of Jehovah's countenance.

Being a Son, the text goes on to tell us that *He had to learn obedience.* Is this not a wonderful thing? As a man, our Savior had to learn. He was of a teachable spirit, and the Lord Himself instructed Him. All God's children go to school, for it is written, "All thy children shall be taught of the LORD" (Isa. 54:13). The lesson is practical—we learn to obey. Our Lord took kindly to this lesson: He did always the things that pleased the Father. This is our time of schooling and discipline, and we are learning to obey, which is the highest and best lesson of all. How near this brings our Lord to us, that He should be a Son and should have to learn! We go to school to Christ and with Christ, and so we feel His fitness to be our compassionate High Priest.

Jesus must also *learn by suffering.* As swimming is to be learned only in the water, so is obedience learned only by actually doing and suffering the divine will. Obedience cannot be learned at the university unless it is at the College of Experience. You must allow the commandment to have its way with you, and then it will educate you. We think when we first come to Christ that we have learned obedience, and assuredly we have in a measure received the spirit by which we obey; but no man knows obedience until he has actually obeyed, both in an active and a passive sense. Even the Lord Jesus must come under the law, honor the law, and suffer the law, or else He cannot learn obedience. Who knows what it is to obey God to the full until he has had to lay aside his own will in the most tender and painful respects? To plead with God for the life of a beloved one and yet to see that life pass away and still bow in reverence—this is to learn obedience. Our Lord as man was made to know by His sufferings what full obedience meant: His was practical, experimental, personal acquaintance with obedience, and in all this He comes very near to us. A Son learning obedience: that is our Lord. May we not joyfully walk with Him in all the rough paths of duty? May we not safely lean on the arm of One who knows every inch of the way?

The Lord Jesus Christ learned this obedience to perfection. The text says, "being made perfect." As a high priest, He is perfect because He has suffered to the end all that was needful to make Him like unto His brethren. He has read the book of obedience quite through. He was not spared one heavy stroke of divine discipline. You and I never go to the end of grief: we are spared the utmost depth, but not so our Lord. The Lord sets us a service proportioned to our strength, but what a service was exacted to the Son of God! Ours is lightened, but not the Savior's. "For it became him, for whom are all things, and by whom are all things, in bringing many sons unto glory, to make the captain of their salvation perfect through sufferings" (Heb. 2:10).

Our Lord learned by suffering mixed with prayer and supplication. His was no unsanctified sorrow. His griefs were baptized with prayer. It cost Him cries and tears to learn the lesson of His sufferings. He never suffered without prayer or prayed without suffering. Supplication and suffering went hand in hand, and in this way our Lord became perfected as the high priest of our profession.

Let us trust ourselves with Him who as a Son knows the training and discipline of sons. Being yourself a son, look up and see what the Elder Brother endured and know that "in that he himself hath suffered being tempted, he is able to succour them that are tempted" (Heb. 2:18). You who are afraid that you never will be the children of God, come and hear your Savior cry as He rises from prayer, "Come unto me, all ye that labour and are heavy laden, and I will give you rest" (Matt. 11:28). Sons of men, why do you wander? Why not come to Him who is made like you? Which way are you looking? Look to Him who suffered in your place and suffered both as your Supplicant and as a Son.

Jesus as a Savior

As a Savior, He is perfect. Being made perfect through suffering, He is able fully to discharge His office. Nothing is lacking in the character and person of Christ for His ability to save to the uttermost. He is a Savior, and a great one. You are wholly lost, but Jesus is perfectly able to save. You are sick, but Jesus is able to perfectly heal. You have gone, perhaps, to the extreme of sin, yet He has gone to the extreme of atonement. In every office essential to your salvation, Jesus is perfect. Nothing is lacking in Him in any one point. However difficult your case may seem, Jesus is equal to it. Made perfect in suffering, He is able to meet the intricacies of your trials and to deliver you in the most complicated emergency.

Henceforth, *He is the author of salvation.* What a suggestive word—the *author* of salvation! Author! How expressive! He is the cause of salvation, the originator, the worker, the producer of salvation. Salvation begins with Christ; salvation is carried on by Christ; salvation is completed by Christ. If a man is the author of a book, it is all his own writing. Salvation has Jesus for its author. If you wish to write a little of the book yourself, then Jesus would not be the author of it, but it would be Jesus and you. We must not intrude into His office. Let the author of salvation complete His own work. Come and accept the salvation that He is waiting to give you. He has finished it, and you cannot add to it; it remains only for you to receive it.

Observe that *it is eternal salvation*: "the author of *eternal* salvation." Jesus does not save us today and leave us to perish tomorrow. He knows what is in man, and so He has prepared nothing less than eternal salvation for man. A salvation that was not eternal would turn out to be no salvation at all. Those whom Jesus saved are saved indeed. Man can be the author of temporary salvation, but only He who is "a priest forever"(Heb. 7:21) can bring in a salvation that endures forever. This reminds me of the word of the prophet: "But Israel shall be saved in the LORD with an everlasting salvation" (Isa. 45:17). I know that whatever the Lord does shall be forever. An eternal salvation is worth having, is it not? Jesus does not give a salvation that lets you fall from grace and perish after all, but a salvation that will keep you to the end. Salvation to eternity and through eternity is provided by Jesus. Love the Lord, all ye His saints, since by His stooping to be perfected as a High Priest, He has been able to bring in for you such a salvation as this.

Furthermore, *His salvation is wide in its range,* for it is to "all them that obey him." Not to some few, not to a little select company here and there, but to "all them that obey him." One of His first commandments is "Repent." Will you obey Him in that and quit your sin? Then He is the author of eternal salvation to you. His great command is, "Believe and live." Will you trust Him, then? For if you do, He is the author of eternal salvation to you. He whom I have tried to describe with all my heart, this blessed sympathetic fellow-sufferer of ours is willing and able to save. Be His, for He has made Himself yours. Seek Him, for He has sought you. Obey Him, for He obeyed for you.

Note that *He is all this forever,* for He is "a high priest after the order of Melchisedec." If you could have seen Him when He came from Gethsemane, you think you could have trusted Him. Trust Him today, for He is a High Priest in an everlasting and perpetual priesthood. He is able to plead for you today, able to put away your sins today. Oh, that God the Holy Spirit may lead you to come and obey Him at once!

Think much of the Son of God, the Lord of heaven and earth, who for our salvation loved and lived and served and suffered. He who made man was made man. As a supplicant, with cries and tears He pleaded with God, even He before whom the hosts of heaven bow adoringly. He has still that tenderness to which He was trained by His sufferings: He bids you now come to Him. You who love Him, approach Him now and read the love that is engraved on His heart. The Man is very near akin to us. Behold how He loves us! He bends to us with eternal salvation in His hands. Believe and live.

Our Lord is called the man of sorrows, for this was His special mark. We might well call Him "a man of holiness," for there is no fault in Him; a man of labors, for He did His Father's business sincerely; a man of eloquence, for never did a man speak like this man. We might very appropriately call Him "the man of love," for never was there greater love than glowed in His heart. Still, conspicuous as all these and many other excellencies were, yet had we gazed upon Christ and been asked afterward what was the most striking characteristic in Him, we should have said His sorrows. The various parts of His character were so singularly harmonious that no one quality dominated so as to become a leading feature. In His moral portrait, the eye is perfect, but so also the mouth; the cheeks are as beds of spices, but the lips also are as lilies, dropping sweet-smelling myrrh. In Peter, you see enthusiasm exaggerated at times into presumption, and in John, love for his Lord would call fire from heaven on His foes. Deficiencies and exaggerations exist everywhere but in Jesus. He is the perfect man, a whole man, the Holy One of Israel. But there was a peculiarity, and it lay in the fact that "his visage was so marred more than any man, and his form more than the sons of men" (Isa. 52:14), through the excessive griefs that continually passed over His spirit. Tears were His insignia, and the cross His ensign. He was the warrior in black armor, and not as now the rider upon the white horse. He was the lord of grief, the prince of pain, the emperor of anguish, a "man of sorrows, and acquainted with grief."

Chapter Four

The Man of Sorrows

A man of sorrows, and acquainted with grief—Isaiah 53:3.

As great as our Lord's sorrows were, they are to be looked upon with sacred triumph. However severe the struggle, the victory has been won; the laboring vessel was severely tossed by the waves, but she has now entered into the desired harbor. Our Savior is no longer in Gethsemane agonizing or upon the cross dying; the crown of thorns has been replaced by many crowns of sovereignty; the nails and the spear have given way to the scepter. Nor is this all, for though the suffering is ended, the blessed results never end. The sowing in tears is followed by a reaping in joy. The bruising of the heel of the woman's seed is well recompensed by the breaking of the serpent's head. It is pleasant to hear of battles fought when a decisive victory has ended war and established peace. So that the double reflection that all the work of suffering is finished by the Redeemer and that He now beholds the success of all His labors, we shall rejoice even while we enter into fellowship with His sufferings.

Let it never be forgotten that the subject of the sorrows of the Savior has proved to be more efficacious for comfort to mourners than any other theme in the compass of revelation or out of it. Even the glories of Christ afford no such consolation to afflicted spirits as the sufferings of Christ. Christ is in all attitudes the consolation of Israel, but He is most so as a man of sorrows. Troubled spirits turn not so much to Bethlehem as to Calvary; they prefer Gethsemane to Nazareth. The afflicted do not so much look for comfort to Christ as He will come a second time in splendor as to Christ as He came the first time, a weary man and full of woes. The passion flower yields us the best perfume; the tree of the cross bleeds the most healing balm. There is no remedy for sorrow beneath the sun like the sorrows of Emmanuel. As Aaron's rod swallowed up all the other rods, so the griefs of Jesus make our griefs disappear. Thus you see that in the black soil of our subject, light is sown for the righteous, light that springs up for those who sit in darkness and in the region of the shadow of death.

"A Man"

Although there is nothing new about the doctrine of the real and actual manhood of the Lord Jesus Christ, there is everything important in it. It is one of those provisions of the Lord's household that, like bread and salt, should be put upon the table at every spiritual meal. We can never meditate too much upon Christ's blessed person as God and as man. Let us reflect that He who is here called a man was certainly "very God of very God," "a man," and "a man of sorrows" and yet at the same time "God over all, blessed for ever." He who was "despised and rejected of men" was beloved and adored by angels, and He from whom men hid their faces in contempt was worshiped by cherubim and seraphim. This is the great mystery of godliness: God was "manifest in the flesh" (1 Tim. 3:16). He who was God and was in the beginning with God was made flesh and dwelt among us. The Highest stooped to become the lowest, and the Greatest took His place among the least. Strange, and needing all our faith to grasp it, yet it is true that He who sat upon the well of Sychar and said, "Give me to drink," was none other than He who dug the channels of the ocean and poured into them the floods. Son of Mary, You are also Son of Jehovah! Man of the substance of Your mother, You are also essential Deity. We worship You this day in spirit and in truth!

Remembering that Jesus Christ is God, we need to recall that His manhood was nonetheless real and substantial. It differed from our own humanity in the absence of sin, but it differed in no other respect. Jesus was born of a woman and grew up as any other little child. His body could be touched and handled, wounded and made to bleed. He was no phantom, but a man of flesh and blood—needing sleep and food and subject to pain—and a man who in the end yielded up His life to death. In body and in soul, the Lord Jesus was perfect man after the order of our manhood, made "in the likeness of sinful flesh" (Rom. 8:3), and we must think of Him under that aspect. Our temptation is to regard the Lord's humanity as something quite different from our own. We are apt to spiritualize it away and not think of Him as really bone of our bone and flesh of our flesh. While we may fancy that we are honoring Christ by such misconceptions, Christ is never honored by that which is not true. He was a man, a real man of our race, the Son of Man: "As the children are partakers of flesh and blood, he also himself likewise took part of the same" (Heb. 2:14). "[He] made himself of no reputation, and took upon him the form of a servant, and was made in the likeness of men" (Phil. 2:7).

This condescending participation in our nature brings the Lord Jesus very near to us in relationship. Inasmuch as He was man, though also God, He was, according to Hebrew law, our kinsman, our next of kin. And it is according to the law that if an inheritance had been lost, it was the right of the next of kin to redeem it. Our Lord Jesus exercised His legal right and, seeing us sold into bondage and our inheritance taken from us, came forward to redeem both us and all our lost estate. It was a blessed thing for us that we had such a kinsman. When Ruth went to glean in the fields of Boaz, it was the most gracious circumstances in her life that Boaz turned out to be her next of kin; and we who have gleaned in the fields of mercy praise the Lord that His only begotten Son is the next of kin to us, our brother, born for adversity. It would not have been consistent with divine justice for any other substitution to have been accepted for us except that of a man. Man sinned, and a man must make reparation for the injury done to the divine honor. The breach of the law was caused by man, and by man must it be repaired. It was not in the power of an angel to have said, "I will suffer for man"—for angelic suffering would have made no amends for human sins. But the man, the matchless man, being the representative man and of right by kinship allowed to redeem, stepped in, suffered what was due, made amends to injured justice, and thereby set us free! Glory be to His blessed name!

And now, since the Lord thus saw in Christ's manhood a suitableness to become our Redeemer, I trust that many who have been under bondage to Satan will see in that same human nature an attraction leading them to approach Him. Because of Jesus, we have not to come to an absolute God or to draw near to a consuming fire. You might well tremble to approach Him whom you have so grievously offended; but there is a man ordained to mediate between you and God, the man Christ Jesus. A holy God will by no means spare the guilty, but look at the Son of Man! He is a man with hands full of blessing, eyes wet with tears of pity, lips overflowing with love, and a heart melting with tenderness. See the gash in His side? Through that wound there is a highway to His heart, and He who needs His compassion may soon excite it.

The way to the Savior's heart is open, and penitent seekers shall never be denied. Why should the most despairing be afraid to approach the Savior? Jesus has taken on the character of the Lamb of God, and I never knew a little child who was afraid of a lamb. I know you may feel sad and trembling, but you need not tremble in *His* presence. If you are weak, your weakness will touch His sympathy, and your mournful inability will be an argument with His abounding mercy. Place yourself by an act of faith beneath the cross of Jesus; look up to Him and say, "Blessed Physician, Your wounds can heal me, Your death for me can make me live, look upon me! You are a man, and You know what man suffers. You are man, and will You let a man sink down to hell who cries to You for help? Will You let a poor unworthy one who longs for mercy be driven into hopeless misery while he cries to You to let Your merits save him?" Fly to Jesus without fear; He waits to save; it is His office to receive sinners and reconcile them to God. May the Holy Spirit lead you to consider the humility of our Lord, and so may you find the door of life, the portal of peace, the gate of heaven!

Every child of God should be comforted by the fact that our Redeemer is one of our race and as our merciful High Priest is able to comfort those who are tempted. The sympathy of Jesus is the next most precious thing to His sacrifice. I bear witness that it has been to me in seasons of great physical pain superlatively comforting to know that in every pang that racks His people the Lord Jesus has a fellow feeling. We are not alone, for one like unto the Son of Man walks the furnace with us. The clouds that float over our sky have beforetime darkened the heavens for Him also.

How completely it takes the bitterness out of grief to know that it once was suffered by Jesus. The Macedonian soldiers, it is said, made long, forced marches that seemed to be beyond the power of mortal endurance, but the reason for their untiring energy lay in Alexander the Great's presence. Alexander was accustomed to walk with and bear their fatigue. If the king himself has been carried like a Persian monarch in a palanquin in the midst of luxury, the soldiers would soon have grown tired. But when they looked upon the king, hungering when they hungered, thirsting when they thirsted, often putting aside the cup of water offered to him and passing it to a fellow soldier who looked more faint than himself, they could not dream of resting. This day, assuredly, we can bear poverty, slander, contempt, or bodily pain, or death itself, because Jesus Christ our Lord has borne it. By His humiliation it shall become our pleasure to be abused for His sake, a fair thing to be made a mockery for Him, an honor to be disgraced, and life itself to surrender life for the sake of such a cause and so precious a Master! May the man of sorrows now appear to us and enable us to bear our sorrows cheerfully. If there is consolation anywhere, surely it is to be found in the delightful presence of the Crucified: "A man shall be as an hiding place from the wind, and a covert from the tempest" (Isa. 32:2).

"A Man of Sorrows"

The expression is intended to be very emphatic, as if Jesus were made up of sorrows and they were constituent elements of His being. Some are men of pleasure, others of wealth, but He was "a man of sorrows." He and sorrow might have changed names. He who saw Him, saw sorrow, and he who would see sorrow, must look on Him. "Behold, and see if there be any sorrow like unto my sorrow, which is done unto me" (Lam. 1:12).

Our Lord is called the man of sorrows, for this was His special mark. We might well call Him "a man of holiness," for there is no fault in Him; a man of labors, for He did His Father's business sincerely; a man of eloquence, for never did a man speak like this man. We might very appropriately call Him "the man of love," for never was there greater love than glowed in His heart. Still, conspicuous as all these and many other excellencies were, yet had we gazed upon Christ and been asked afterward what was the most striking characteristic in Him, we should have said His sorrows.

The various parts of His character were so singularly harmonious that no one quality dominated so as to become a leading feature. In His moral portrait, the eye is perfect, but so also the mouth; the cheeks are as beds of spices, but the lips also are as lilies, dropping sweet-smelling myrrh. In Peter, you see enthusiasm exaggerated at times into presumption, and in John, love for his Lord would call fire from heaven on His foes. Deficiencies and exaggerations exist everywhere but in Jesus. He is the perfect man, a whole man, the Holy One of Israel. But there was a peculiarity, and it lay in the fact that "his visage was so marred more than any man, and his form more than the sons of men" (Isa. 52:14), through the excessive griefs that continually passed over His spirit. Tears were His insignia, and the cross His ensign. He was the warrior in black armor, and not as now the rider upon the white horse. He was the lord of grief, the prince of pain, the emperor of anguish, a "man of sorrows, and acquainted with grief."

Is not the title of "man of sorrows" given to our Lord by way of *eminence*? He was not only sorrowful but also preeminent among the sorrowful. All men have a burden to bear, but His was heaviest of all. Who is there of our race who is free from sorrows? Search the whole earth, and everywhere the thorn and thistle will be found, and these have wounded every person ever born. High in the lofty place of the earth there is sorrow, for the royal widow weeps for her lord: down in the cottage where we imagine that nothing but content can reign, a thousand bitter tears are shed over loss and oppression. In the sunniest heights, the serpent creeps among the flowers; in the most fertile regions, poisons flourish as well as wholesome herbs. There is sorrow on the sea and sadness on the land. But in this common experience, the "firstborn among many brethren" (Rom. 8:29) has more than a double portion, His cup is more bitter, His baptism more deep than the rest of the family. Common sufferers must give place, for none can match with Him in woe. Ordinary mourners may be content to rend their garments, but He Himself is rent in His affliction; they sip at sorrow's bow, but He drains it dry. He who was the most obedient Son smarted most under the rod when He was stricken of God and afflicted; no other of the smitten ones have sweat great drops of blood or cried out in bitter anguish, "My God, my God, why hast thou forsaken me?" (Matt. 27:46).

The reasons for this superior sorrow may be found in the fact that with His sorrow there was no mixture of sin. Sin deserves sorrow, but it also blunts the edge of grief by rendering the soul untender and unsympathetic. We do not tremble at the sinner's doom or become alarmed at sin as Jesus did. His was a perfect nature that, because it knew no sin, was not in its element amid sorrow but was like a land bird driven out to sea by a gale. To the convict the jail is his home, but to an innocent man a prison is misery, and everything about it is strange and foreign. Our Lord's pure nature was peculiarly sensitive to any contact with sin; we, alas, by the fall, have lost much of that feeling. In proportion as we are sanctified, sin becomes the source of wretchedness to us; Jesus being perfect, every sin pained Him much more than it would any of us. David's prayer is full of agony when he cries, "Gather not my soul with sinners, nor my life with bloody men" (Ps. 26:9). But the perfect Jesus, what a grief the sight of sin must have caused Him! We grow callous as our hearts go on sinning, but our Lord was like a man whose flesh was delicately sensitive to every touch of sin. He could see sin where we cannot see it and feel its heinousness as we cannot feel it. There was therefore more to give Him, and He was more capable of being grieved.

Side by side with His painful sensitiveness of the evil of sin was His gracious tenderness toward the sorrows of others. If we could know and enter into all the griefs of those around us, we would be of all men most miserable. There are heartbreaks that, could they find a tongue, would fill our heart with agony. We hear of poverty, see disease, observe bereavement, mark distress, and note that men are passing into the grave on their descent to hell, but somehow or other, either these become such common things that they do not stir us, or else we gradually harden to them. The Savior was always moved to sympathy with another's griefs, for His love was ever at floodtide. All men's sorrows were His sorrows. His heart was so large that it was inevitable that He should become "a man of sorrows."

We recall that besides this our Savior had a peculiar relationship to sin. He was not merely afflicted with the sight of it and saddened by perceiving its effects on others, but sin was actually laid upon Him, and He was Himself numbered with the transgressors. Therefore He was called to bear the terrible blows of divine justice and suffered unknown, immeasurable agonies. His Godhead strengthened Him to suffer, or else manhood would have failed Him. The wrath whose power no man knows spent itself on Him: "It pleased the LORD to bruise him; he hath put him to grief" (Isa. 53:10). Behold the man and mark how vain it would be to seek His equal sorrow.

The title of "man of sorrows" was also given to our Lord to indicate the *constancy* of His afflictions. He changed His place of abode, and He always lodged with sorrow. Sorrow wove His swaddling bands, and sorrow spun His winding sheet. Born in a stable, sorrow received Him, and only on the cross at His last breathe did sorrow part with Him. His disciples might forsake Him, but His sorrows would not leave Him. He was often alone without a man, but never alone without a grief. From the hour of His baptism in Jordan to the time of His baptism in the pains of death, He always wore the sable robe and was "a man of sorrows."

He also was a "man of sorrows" for the *variety* of His woes. He was a man not of *sorrow* only but of *sorrows*. All the sufferings of the body and of the soul were known to Him, the sorrows of the man who actively struggles to obey, the sorrows of the man who sits still and passively endures. The sorrows of the lofty He knew, for He was the King of Israel; the sorrows of the poor He knew, for He had nowhere to lay His head. Sorrows relative and sorrows personal, sorrows mental and sorrows spiritual, sorrows of all kinds and degrees assailed Him. Affliction emptied its quiver upon Him, making His heart the target for all conceivable woes.

Our Lord was a man of sorrows as to His poverty. You who are in need, your need is not so extreme as His; He had nowhere to lay His head, but you have at least some humble roof to shelter you. No one denies you a cup of water, but He sat upon the well of Samaria in great thirst. We read more than once that He hungered. His toil was so great that He was constantly weary, constantly called upon by those in need, with nothing of earthly comfort to make that life endurable. And He knew what it meant to lament around the open grave, feeling the heartrendings of bereavement. Jesus wept as He stood at the tomb of Lazarus.

Perhaps the bitterest of His sorrows were those that were connected with His gracious work. He came as the Messiah sent of God on a mission of love, and men rejected His claims. When He went to His own city, where He had grown up, and announced himself, they would have cast Him headlong down the hill. It is a hard thing to come on such an errand and be met with such ingratitude as this.

Nor did they stay at cold rejection; they then proceeded to derision and ridicule. There was no name of contempt that they did not pour upon Him, and afterward they proceeded to falsehood, slander, and blasphemy. He was a drunken man, they said; hear this, you angels, and be astonished! They said He was in league with Beelzebub and had a devil and was mad, whereas He had come to destroy the works of the devil! They charged Him with every crime that their malice could suggest. There was not a word He spoke but what they would find in His words some misrepresentation. And all the while He was doing nothing but seeking their good. When He was sincere against their vices, it was out of pity for their souls. If He condemned their sins, it was because their sins would destroy them. But His zeal against sin was always tempered with love for the souls of men. Was there ever a man so full of goodwill to others who received such disgraceful treatment from those He longed to serve?

As He proceeded in His life, His sorrows multiplied. He preached but found men's hearts were hard, and He was grieved for the hardness of their hearts. He pleaded with them and declared His love but received a hatred remorseless and fiendish. Slighted love has griefs of peculiar poignancy, but His griefs were immeasurable. Such love as the love of Jesus brought sorrow, not that men injured Him but that they destroyed themselves. He could lament over the city of Jerusalem for their suicidal rejection of His grace. These were among the sorrows that He bore.

While He found some solace with the few companions whom He had gathered around Him, it appears that He found even more sorrow in their company. They learned slowly, and what they did learn, they forgot; what they remembered, they did not practice; and what they practiced at one time, they belied at another. They were miserable comforters for the man of sorrows. His was a lonely life, meaning that even when He was with His followers, He was alone. He said to them once, "Could ye not watch with me one hour?" (Matt. 26:40), but He might have said the same to them all the hours of their lives, for even if they sympathized with Him to the utmost of their capacity, they could not enter into such griefs as His. The Savior, from the very dignity of His nature, must suffer alone. The mountainside with Christ upon it seems to me to be a suggestive symbol of His earthly life. His great soul lived in vast solitudes, sublime and terrible, and there amid a midnight of trouble His spirit communed with the Father, with no one able to accompany Him into the dark valleys and gloomy ravines of His unique experience. And at the last, every follower forsook Him—one denied Him, and another betrayed Him.

In the last, crowning sorrows of His life, there came upon Him the penal afflictions of God, the chastisement of our peace that was upon Him. He was arrested in the garden of Gethsemane by God's officers before the officers of the Jews had come near to Him. There on the ground He knelt and wrestled till the bloody sweat started from every pore, and His soul was "exceeding sorrowful, even unto death" (Matt. 26:38). He went from there to be treated with mingled scorn and cruelty before the judgment seat. When they had almost murdered Him with scourging, they brought Him forth and said, "Behold the man." Their malice was not satisfied; they must go further yet and nail Him to His cross and mock Him while fever parched His mouth and made Him feel as if His body was dissolved to dust. He calls out for drink and is mocked with vinegar. But remember that the sharpest scourging and severest griefs were all within, while the hand of God bruised Him and the iron rod of justice broke Him, as it were, upon the wheel.

He was fitly named a "man of sorrows." I feel that I cannot find words worthy of my theme, yet I know that embellishments of language would degrade rather than adorn the agonies of my Lord. There let the cross stand sublime in its simplicity! It needs no decoration. If I had wreaths of choicest flowers to hang upon it, I would gladly place them there, and if instead of garlands of flowers, each flower could be a gem of priceless worth, I would consider that the cross deserved the whole. But as I have none of these, I rejoice that the cross alone, in its naked simplicity, needs nothing from a mortal pen. Turn to your bleeding Savior. Continue gazing upon Him, and find the "man of sorrows" your Lord and your God.

"Acquainted with Grief"

With grief He had an *intimate* acquaintance. He did not know merely what it was in others, but it came home to Himself. We have sometimes felt grief, but the Lord felt it more intensely than other men in His innermost soul. He, beyond us all, was conversant with this black letter lore. He knew the secret of the heart that refuses to be comforted. He had sat at grief's table, eaten of its black bread, and dipped His morsel in her vinegar. By the waters of Marah He dwelt and knew the bitter well.

It was a *continuous* acquaintance. He did not call at grief's house to take a sip now and then, but the cup was always in His hand, and the ashes were always mingled with His bread. Not only forty days in the wilderness did Jesus fast; the world was ever a wilderness to Him, and His life was one long Lent. I do not mean that He was not a happy man, for down deep in His soul, benevolence always supplied a living spring of joy to Him. There was a joy into which we are one day to enter—the "joy of our Lord"—the "joy that was set before him" for which "he endured the cross, despising the shame" (Heb. 12:2). But that does not at all take away from the fact that His acquaintance with grief was continuous and intimate beyond that of any man who ever lived. It was indeed a *growing* acquaintance with grief, for every step took Him deeper down into the grim shades of sorrow. As there is a progress in the teaching of Christ and in the life of Christ, so there is also in the griefs of Christ. The tempest lowered darker and darker. His sun rose in a cloud, but it set in congregated horrors of heaped-up night till, in a moment, the clouds were suddenly rent asunder and, as a loud voice proclaimed "It is finished," a glorious morning dawned where all expected an eternal night.

Remember that this acquaintance of Christ with grief was *voluntary* for our sakes. He never would have known a grief at all, and at any moment He might have said farewell to grief. He could have returned in an instant to the royalties of heaven, but He would not. He remained to the end, out of love to us, grief's acquaintance.

So let us admire the superlative love of Jesus. O love, love, what have you done? What have you not done! You are omnipotent in suffering. Few of us can bear pain; perhaps fewer still can bear misrepresentation, slander, and ingratitude. These are horrible hornets that sting as with fire. Men have been driven to madness by cruel scandals that have distilled from venomous tongues. Christ throughout life bore these and other sufferings. Let us love Him as we think of how much He must have loved us. Get your souls saturated with the love of Christ. Let them soak in His love till, like a sponge, you drink into your own self the love of Jesus. Admire the power of His love, and then pray that you may have a love somewhat like it in power.

Jesus was "a man of sorrows, and acquainted with grief." But many of His disciples live for themselves. There are rich men who call themselves saints and are thought to be so, whose treasures are hoarded for themselves and their families. There are men of ability who believe that they are bought with Christ's blood, yet their ability is all spent on other things and none upon their Lord. Perhaps you must confess that you are doing nothing for Christ. Do not let this day pass until you have begun to do something for your Lord. By the nail prints of His hand, labor for Jesus! By His wounded feet, run to His help! By the scar in His side, give Him your heart! By that sacred head, once pierced with thorns, yield Him your thoughts! By the shoulder that bore the scourges, bend your entire strength to His service! Give yourself, your heart, soul, and strength to Jesus! Live in His service and die in His service! You who love Him and fight for Him, you are summoned to the front. Hasten to the conflict and charge home for the "man of sorrows"! Make this the cry of battle today! By the cross that bore Him and by the heavy cross He bore, by His deadly agony and by the agony of His life, I cry, "forward, for the man of sorrows!" Write this on your wealth, bind this inscription on all your possessions: "This belongs to the man of sorrows." Live for Him and be ready to die for Him, and the Lord accept you for the "man of sorrows" sake.

Real strength is the backbone of meekness. The angry are weak, the patient are strong; the infinite heart of Jesus is a meek heart, partly because it is infinite. And I have noticed, too, that really great men are lowly men; at any rate they are only great as far as they are lowly. When a man is fond of dignity, pomp, and show, he is a second-rate man and an essentially little man. Those who stick out for minute points of honor and respect are the very small men. The man who must have all his titles written after his name shows that he feels he needs them. The more eminent a man becomes, the plainer his name becomes in men's mouths. The greatest men among us in the state are seldom or never called even by their full names and honors but are known by the shortest designations. The greater a man is, the less state he cares for. All the world over, the man who wants to be thought great is essentially little, and he, who for the good of others is ready for any service, has the elements of greatness in his character. The Lord Jesus Christ is so infinitely great that none can add to His glory, and therefore He is surpassingly low, too. We are too proud to seek the conversion of the prostitute, but He was not; He went to Samaria to find her and talk to her. We are too great to speak to the babes, but He said, "Suffer little children, and forbid them not, to come unto me" (Matt. 19:14). It is a delightful thought that He should be so great and yet so lowly, and there is an intimate connection between the two great facts.

Chapter Five

The Heart of Jesus

I am meek and lowly in heart—Matthew 11:29.

IT IS VERY REMARKABLE that the only passage in the whole New Testament in which the heart of Jesus is distinctly mentioned is the one before us. Of course, there are passages in which His heart is intended, as when the soldier with a spear pierced Jesus' side; but this passage is unique as to the actual mention of the *kardia* or heart of Jesus by a distinct word. Several passages in the Old Testament refer to our divine Lord, such as "Reproach hath broke my heart; and I am full of heaviness" (Ps. 69:20) and that notable one, "My heart is like wax; it is melted in the midst of my bowels" (Ps. 22:14). But in the New Testament, this is the only passage that speaks of the heart of Jesus Christ, and therefore we will weigh it with all the more care. We shall have two things carefully to do: first, we will *consider the description here given of the heart of Jesus,* and second, we will *labor to obey the exhortations that are connected with the description.* For both these matters we shall need the rich assistance of the Holy Spirit, and I pray that He will take the precious things of Jesus and show them to us, shining upon the sacred heart of our loving Lord.

The Heart of Jesus

It consists of two adjectives: "I am *meek* and *lowly* in heart." There is no pomp or display in either of the qualities mentioned. They both belong to the gentle order of virtues and are but little esteemed among the princes of this world and their warriors.

The first word is *meek*. It is used in the third beatitude: "Blessed are the meek: for they shall inherit the earth" (Matt. 5:5), and by Peter when speaking of "the ornament of a meek and quiet spirit, which is in the sight of God of great price" (1 Pet. 3:4). Of our Lord also it is said: "Behold, thy King cometh unto thee, meek, and sitting upon an ass, and a colt the foal of an ass" (Matt. 21:5). The original word has the significations of "mild, gentle, soft, meek." Such is the heart of Christ. And you will observe that Jesus Christ says this concerning Himself: "I am meek and lowly in heart." There are points of character that a man could not properly declare concerning himself or it might speak of self praise, but the virtue of meekness was of old so little esteemed that a man might claim it without being suspected of seeking acclaim.

It is amazing that Moses recorded in Numbers 12 the fact that he was remarkable for meekness: "Now the man Moses was very meek, above all the men which were upon the face of the earth" (vs. 3). It has been thought by some that this verse was inserted later and could not have been written by Moses, but I strongly object to this supposition. I believe that Moses, guided by infallible inspiration, wrote that description of himself for our example and was utterly free from any vainglory in so doing, just as our Lord in all lowliness here spoke concerning Himself. Meekness never seeks its own, and when it asserts itself, it is always with an eye to the benefit of others; therefore none can tell it to be silent. For a man to boast before his adversaries, "I am wise" or "I am strong," would be vainglory. But to say to them, "I am meek," would be no boasting but a sacred argument for peace, a plea for gentleness and quiet.

Our Savior, who never sought the praise of man, says of Himself, "I am meek," because He desired to remove the fears of those who trembled to approach Him and would win the allegiance of those who feared to become His followers lest His service should prove too severe. He, in effect, cried, "Come to Me, you offending men, you who feel your unworthiness, you who think that your transgressions may provoke My anger; come to Me, for I am meek." It would be no pride for a man to say, "I am strong," if he would thereby convince a drowning person to trust him for the saving of his life. Neither would it be wrong for a person to say, as a physician does say, "I am wise in medicine," in order to lead a dying person to take the medicine that he felt sure would heal the person. We may and must assert ourselves and confess those qualities that are truly ours if, by so doing, as did Jesus, a great benefit may be bestowed upon others. Jesus knew that this gentle attribute would silence fear and lead the timid to approach Him and learn of Him.

The other adjective is *lowly*. This is the word that is translated in the memorable song of Mary, *low degree*. "He hath put down the mighty from their seats, and exalted them of low degree" (Luke 1:52). It is also used in Romans 12:16, where Paul says, "Mind not high things, but condescend to men of low estate." So again in 2 Corinthians 7:6, where it is rendered differently: "God, that comforteth those that are cast down." In James 4:6, the word is translated *humble*: "God resisteth the proud, but giveth grace unto the humble." If you turn to any Greek lexicon, you will find that the word does not signify merely what the Scriptures translate it by, but since the Greeks were a warlike people, a proud people, and thought it foul scorn to patiently endure an insult, the word that we translate by *lowliness* they would understand to mean *keeping near the ground, vile, contemptible.*

And so our Savior has chosen to describe His own heart by a word that unregenerate men would thus misinterpret. Even now, a man who will not fight but has learned to suffer wrong without resenting it is thought by certain people to be lacking in spirit and worthy of contempt. That lowly grace that the world calls contemptible Jesus claims as being His own special quality. He is not lofty, ambitious, proud, and haughty. He dwelt with the humble and contrite; He associated with men of low estate, such as the ungodly would look down upon as utterly beneath regard. He made Himself of no reputation and took upon Him the form of a servant. When He was reviled, He reviled not in return. He did not strive or cry or cause His voice to be heard in the streets; a bruised reed He did not break, and the smoking flax He did not quench (Isa. 42:3). Thus was He *meek and lowly in heart.*

This description of the heart of Christ may be understood as opposed first to quickness of anger. Meek men bear many provocations. Some men explode at a single spark; if you do but even seem to pay them disrespect, they are indignant in a moment. But Christ said, "I am meek. I can pardon your ingratitude and disrespect. I can forgive your profanity, your blasphemy, your insult, your scorn, your enmity, your malice, for I am meek." Even when put to a cruel death, He muttered no curse and threatened no revenge. "Slow to anger, and plenteous in mercy" (Ps. 103:8), like His Father, is the Son of the Highest.

Meekness and lowliness are also opposed to haughtiness of spirit. Jesus did not seek the empty glories of pomp and state; neither did He desire honor from men. He did not speak proudly to those around Him and domineer over them or exercise lordship over them as the princes of the Gentiles do. He was approachable, easy to be reached, and ready to be entreated. The poor and the sick could easily move His heart to pity and His hand to help. He was called the friend of publicans and sinners, and of Him it was said, "This man receiveth sinners, and eateth with them" (Luke 15:2). As a teacher, Jesus was meek and lowly in heart, and therein was the very opposite of the scribes. If you saw a Pharisee in Christ's day, you would have seen the incarnation of pride. By his very name, the Pharisee professed to be a select person, and in dress, manner, and conversation he set himself up to be some great one. A Pharisee would not come near a sinner if he could help it, passing the sinner in the street as though he were a dog. But Christ was gentle and willing to associate with the vilest of the vile and the lowest of the low, for He was "lowly in heart."

The expression of the text is also opposed to that pretended meekness and mock lowliness that has at times imposed itself upon the world. It is true our Savior was meek and lowly, for even in His greatest pomp He rode upon a colt, the foal of an ass, and not upon a horse, which indicated state. He was ever lowly in manner and behavior, and though He could flame and flash with sacred boldness and speak words that burn in His holy indignation against hypocrisy, when He uttered the glad message of the gospel He was very gentle, even as a nurse with her child. Yet the meekness and lowliness of Christ were not things of manner and of word alone: He was so in His heart. He was not of those who pretend humility to secure power. It is said of Thomas à Becket that he affected the greatest lowliness and humility, and for this reason he washed the feet of thirteen beggars every morning; but yet he was arrogance itself and lorded it over his king. He was the proudest of the proud, though he pretended to be the humblest of the humble.

Many men have concealed inordinate pride beneath the crouching manner, mimicking humility while harboring arrogance. While their spirit has been full of imperial despotism, they have pretended to be the friends of the people. Not so our truthful Master. To Him association with the poor and sinful was no pretense of condescension. He was already on their level in intense sympathy with their sorrows. His heart was with the common people. He did not force Himself down from a natural haughtiness to a constrained contact with the lowly, but He became a real friend of sinners and a willing companion of the needy. He rejoiced in spirit when He said, "I thank thee, O Father, Lord of heaven and earth, that thou hast hid these things from the wise and prudent, and hast revealed them unto babes" (Luke 10:21). His meek and lowly heart was by its very nature to be clear of anger and pride, passion, and enmity. Thus from its opposites we see more clearly the meaning of the text.

It will further help us if we consider that the words employed here include first, a readiness on the part of Christ to pardon all past offenses. "Come to Me, you sinners, for however much you may have offended in the past, I am meek and easily entreated. I am ready to forgive and forget. My very heart says it, for My heart is full of tenderness and compassion for you. I have borne much from you and can bear still more. I will be mindful of your weaknesses and forgetful of your transgressions. I will not be so grieved by your rebellions as to cast you out if you come to Me." Jesus is long-suffering, pitiful, and ready to forgive; like His Father, He passes by transgression, iniquity, and sin because He delights in mercy.

But the words include also a willingness to endure yet further offenses. "I am meek" means "not only do I forget the past, but I am ready to bear with you still, though you should still offend Me. Though you are ungrateful and give me unkindness for My love, I will endure it all. Come to Me, although you cannot hope that your future character will be perfect. I will help you to struggle into holiness and be patient with your failures. If you come to Me, I am prepared to forgive you unto seventy times seven, as often as you shall err, so often will I restore you. As frequently as you shall grieve Me, so frequently will I forgive you. If you take my yoke, I will not be angry if sometimes it appears heavy to you. If you learn of Me, I will not be perturbed if you prove to be a slow learner. I will bear with you in the present and in the future." Beloved, what a heart Jesus has to receive sinners in this divine manner!

As to the second word, "I am lowly in heart"; that means "I am willing to receive the lowest and the poorest among you; the most obscure, despised, and ignorant, I welcome to My salvation. O you who labor and are heavy laden, I shall not feel in your coming to Me that you are presuming and that your company is a dishonor to Me. I shall not say to you, go away because I have chosen the company of kings and princes, of philosophers and divines, of the wealthy and the witty." No, Jesus covets not the so-called aristocracy but seeks after men of all ranks. The poor have the gospel preached to them. Some of His professed ministers have looked down upon the working class, but their Master said, "Come unto me, all ye that labour" (Matt. 11:28). Do not stand back because you are of low estate, for Jesus is of a lowly heart. Come to Him, you who feel like offcasts, outcasts, and men of no caste at all, for Jesus also was rejected by His brethren. Ye who are despised, come to Him who was despised of men. You who are homeless, come to Him who had nowhere to lay His head. You who are needy, come to Him who hungered and thirsted. You who are lost, come to the Son of Man, who is come to seek and to save that which was lost.

His lowliness means this also, that as He is willing to receive the lowest, so He is willing to do the very lowest and most menial service for those who come to Him; willing to bear their burdens, willing to wash their feet, willing to purge them from their sins in His own blood. Jesus waits to be gracious and delights to save to the uttermost those who come unto God by Him. For sinners He has performed feats of lowly love, for He has borne their sin and their shame, their iniquities, and their sicknesses. He willingly stooped to the lowest position to save the lowest of men. My heart glows within me while I am telling you these things about my own dear Lord and Master, "whose shoe's latchet I am not worthy to unloose"(John 1:27). Jesus has, in these two words, as with two masterly strokes of the pencil, given us a perfect picture of His dear, gentle face; no, not of His face, but of His inmost heart. How I wonder that we are not all in love with Him. "Meek and lowly in heart!" These are two beauties, which to sinners' eyes, when sinners know themselves, are the most lovely and fascinating attributes, such as charm their fears and chain their hearts. He who has eyes to see, let him look there, and looking, let him love.

To set forth these words a little more, I beg you to recall that they are enhanced in value if we reflect who it is that speaks them of Himself. Remember it is the Lord God, the Son of the Highest, who says, "I am meek and lowly in heart." At first these words speak to me with a still, small voice and make me very glad. Then, like Moses at the bush, I draw near to it, but lest I should be too bold and grow irreverent, it changes its tone, and I hear peal upon peal of thunder issuing from it as I listen to the words: "I am." Can you not hear in those words the incommunicable name Jehovah, the Self-existent One? Yet, as I listen awestruck to that thunder's crash and fear lest it might foretell a tempest and precede destruction, I feel the soft drops of eternal mercy fall upon my brow and hear again the gentle voice of the Mediator saying, "Meek and lowly in heart." Jehovah Jesus is gentle, tender, and condescending. What a divine blending of glory and grace! It is marvelous! Words cannot set it forth! Omnipotent, yet lowly! Eternal God, yet a patient sufferer! King of kings and Lord of lords, yet "meek and lowly in heart"!

Remember well that He who spoke these words is He who said, "All things are delivered unto me of my Father" (Matt. 11:27). Yes, He is possessor of all things, and yet He says, "I am meek and lowly in heart." It is hard to be a man of power and yet to be meek, to be a king and to order things after your own will and yet to be lowly, to be master of all and to suffer with patience the scoffs and reproaches of those who are not worthy to be put among the dogs of your flock. To have all things delivered to Him by God and yet to be so meek as to endure all manner of contradiction of sinners against Himself, to allow sinners to spit in His face, to pluck His hair, and to scourge Him cruelly. This is matchless and unparalleled meekness and lowliness of heart! Yet such was Jesus Christ as God Almighty and as man most lowly. Having an infinite mediatorial power, with all things delivered to Him, yet was our Redeemer "meek and lowly in heart."

Call to mind also that Jesus said, "the Father...hath committed all judgment unto the Son" (John 5:22). If it were your business and mine, as it is not, to exercise judgment and to be the universal censors, I warrant you it would be a superlative difficulty to be able to retain a meek and lowly heart. But Jesus Christ is universal Judge.

His eyes, like flames of fire, discern between the precious and the vile, burning up the stubble and purifying the gold, and yet, though ruler of all mankind and soon to come upon His throne to judge both angels and men, He could say in the days of His flesh, "I am meek and lowly in heart." These are very wonderful words. I do not know whether you catch the contrast. If you do not, it is my fault in not being able to state it, for it is surpassingly striking. A divine being, superlative in power and commissioned to judge mankind and yet, for all that, "meek and lowly in heart."

It is most possible that the very reason of His meekness and lowliness may lie somewhere in His glorious greatness, though it may seem a paradox, for who are the meekest in the world but those who are truly strong? You shall pass down the road and a yelping dog will bark at you, but a powerful bull feeds on in peace. Real strength is the backbone of meekness. The angry are weak, the patient are strong; the infinite heart of Jesus is a meek heart, partly because it is infinite. And I have noticed, too, that really great men are lowly men; at any rate they are only great as far as they are lowly. When a man is fond of dignity, pomp, and show, he is a second-rate man and an essentially little man. Those who stick out for minute points of honor and respect are the very small men. The man who must have all his titles written after his name shows that he feels he needs them. The more eminent a man becomes, the plainer his name becomes in men's mouths. The greatest men among us in the state are seldom or never called even by their full names and honors but are known by the shortest designations. The greater a man is, the less state he cares for. All the world over, the man who wants to be thought great is essentially little, and he, who for the good of others is ready for any service, has the elements of greatness in his character. The Lord Jesus Christ is so infinitely great that none can add to His glory, and therefore He is surpassingly low, too. We are too proud to seek the conversion of the prostitute, but He was not; He went to Samaria to find her and talk to her. We are too great to speak to the babes, but He said, "Suffer little children, and forbid them not, to come unto me" (Matt. 19:14). It is a delightful thought that He should be so great and yet so lowly, and there is an intimate connection between the two great facts.

Our blessed Lord proved throughout His life the truth of what He asserted by saying, "I am meek and lowly in heart." He stated what His biography, if it is studied rightly, most fully bears out. When He came to earth, His first advent was to a stable and to a humble woman's breast. His youth was spent in a carpenter's shop, and when some gleamings of His superlative wisdom were seen in the temple, yet He went back with His mother and His reputed father and was subject to them. Throughout His life His associations were with the poor. He never put on fancy clothing or paraded in the courts of princes. Herod might be anxious to see something of Jesus, but Christ never went to the palace to flatter Herod or to amuse his curiosity. Jesus was quite content to be with Peter and James and John, humble fishermen as they were. His tenderness toward children was always remarkable. His gentleness toward all that approached Him was most memorable. Whom did He ever spurn? To whom did He ever speak in tones of pride. When was He ever irritated? Did He not bear insults in silence? Did He not answer craftiness with wisdom? Was not mercy His only reply to malice? Even in His death His silence before His enemies was His lowliness, and His prayer for His murderers was His meekness. While "despised and rejected of men," He was evermore their friend and lover, returning good for all their evil. He was indeed "meek and lowly in heart."

Obeying Christ's Commands

There are three commands: "Come unto me," "take my yoke upon you," and "learn of me."

First, I have great pleasure in declaring that every reader who is heavy laden and laboring is invited to *come* to Christ; and you are persuaded to do so because He is meek. No matter what your age is or how long you have neglected Jesus or however great your transgressions or whether you have refused His mercy a thousand times, yet He says to come. All this He will forgive, for He is meek, and He invites all guilty sinners to look into His heart and see if they can discover anything like vengeance or implacable wrath. He does not repel even blasphemers. He says, "Come as you are. You are unfit and unworthy, yet still come. I know what you are, I have considered you. I know that your frame is dust and that your nature is sinful, yet still I say, come, for I am able to keep you from falling."

To meet another set of objections, which arise not so much from sinfulness as from a sense of insignificance, Jesus declares, "I

am lowly in heart." Jesus loves the poorest, the wretched, the ignorant, the unknown, the disgraced, the sick, and the troubled. Jesus
rejects no seeking soul. None are beneath Him: His love can
descend lower than you have ever fallen. If you lie between the
jaws of hell, Jesus can pluck you out. It is delightful to my soul to
tell these glad tidings to you. Has the tender love of Jesus no
beauty in your eyes? Nothing should charm you and encourage
you more. Jesus, by His own lips, speaks to you: "Come unto me,
all ye that labor and are heavy laden." May His Spirit lead you.
Come and trust the Savior; come and bow at His dear pierced feet;
come and take from His wounded hands the boundless mercies
that He delights to give. Come and look into His face, for it beams
with love and welcomes you to His friendship.

The second command to obey is to "take my yoke upon you."
This is for you. Obey Christ, for He is no tyrannical master. It is
very easy to serve a man who is lowly and meek. It is very difficult,
I should think, to be continually employed by a person who is too
haughty to speak to you, whose commands are intolerant, and
who, if you do not fulfill them to the letter, will scold you in furi-
ous language. It must be hard to be a servant to a hard master. But,
oh, to serve Jesus is to serve one whose service is perfect freedom,
who is ever lenient toward our faults, who forgives as soon as we
offend, and if grieved by us is only grieved because we injure ourselves. Who would not obey Jesus? Who would not wait upon so
kind a Prince?

The third command is to "learn of me, for I am meek and lowly
in heart." This is a lesson that I want to learn: to be meek! We are
not all meek, and some of us who may appear to be meek perhaps
owe it rather to a softness of nature than to a sweetness of grace;
but the true meekness is that which grace gives. Matthew Henry
says that there are only three men in the Bible whose faces are said
to have shone—Moses, Jesus, and Stephen—and all these were
meek men. God will not make angry men's faces shine. If anything
can put a divine glow on a Christian's face, it is a readiness to forgive. If you are ready to forgive, you possess one of the sweetest
beauties of the Redeemer's character. It is wonderful, the power of
meekness, if we would but believe it. There is no power in anger
after all. "For the wrath of man worketh not the righteousness of
God" (James 1:20). Stoop to conquer; submit to overcome. Nothing
conquers like meekness, not the meekness that is pretended, but

real gentleness. Of all things in the world, I think the most sickening is the pretense of forgiving a person when you yourself are the individual who committed the offense. The sanctimonious pretense of meekness when you are justly upbraided is detestable. May God grant us grace to find peace by getting rid of anger, for only by meekness shall you find peace unto your souls. You cannot be at peace while you are harsh and severe and ready to resent every small injury.

The other word is "lowly in heart." This is one of the things every believer should learn from Christ. Augustine was once asked what the most essential thing there was in religion. He replied, "The first essential is humility, the second is humility, and the third is humility." There is more than that essential, but at the same time in a perfect Christian character, one of the rarest but at the same time one of the most precious pearls is humility. The lowliest Christ is the loveliest Christian. A full man is a humble man; a proud man is an empty man. Conceit means weakness; lowliness of heart is strength. Jesus Christ was strong and yet meek, great and yet lowly. Oh, that we might learn that lesson from Him and be "meek and lowly in heart."

The figure our Lord used is full of meaning, for in the next place, the hen is to her chicks the source of comfort. It is a cold night, and they would be frozen if they remained outside. But the hen calls them in, and when they are under her wings, they derive warmth from their mother's breast. It is wonderful, the care of a hen for her little ones. She will sit so carefully and keep her wings so widely spread that they may all be housed. What a cabin, what a palace it is for the young chicks to get there under the mother's wings! The snow may fall or the rain come pelting down, but the wings of the hen protect the chicks. If you come to Christ, you shall have not only safety but also comfort. I speak what I have experienced. There is a deep, sweet comfort about hiding yourself away in God, for when troubles come wave upon wave, blessed is the man who has a God to give him mercy upon mercy. When affliction or bereavement comes, when loss of property comes, when sickness comes in your own body, there is nothing wanted but your God. Apart from Him, ten thousand things cannot satisfy you or give you comfort. There, let them all go; but if God is yours and you hide away under His wings, you are as happy in Him as the chicks are beneath the hen.

Chapter Six

"I Would, But Ye Would Not"

O Jerusalem, Jerusalem, thou that killest the prophets, and stonest them which are sent unto thee, how often would I have gathered thy children together, even as a hen gathereth her chickens under her wings, and ye would not!—Matthew 23:37.

THIS IS NOT and could not be the language of a mere man. It would be utterly absurd for any man to say that he would have gathered the inhabitants of a city together, "even as a hen gathereth her chickens under her wings." Besides, the language implies that for many centuries, by the sending of the prophets and by many other warnings, God would often have gathered the children of Jerusalem together in this manner. Christ could not have gathered those people if He had been only a man. If His life began at Bethlehem, this would be an absurd statement; but as the Son of God, ever loving the sons of men, ever desirous of the good of Israel, He could say that in sending the prophets, even though they were stoned and killed, He had again and again shown His desire to bless His people till He could truly say, "How often would I have gathered thy children together!" Some who have found difficulties in this lament have said that it was the language of Christ the man. I beg to put in a very decided negative to that; it is, and it must be, the utterance of the Son of Man, the Son of God, the Christ in His complex person as human and divine.

You could not fully understand this passage from any point of view unless you believed it to be the language of one who was both God and man.

This verse shows also that the ruin of men lies with themselves. Christ puts it very plainly: "*I would; but ye would not.*" That is a truth about which I hope we have never had any question. We hold tenaciously that salvation is all of grace, but we also believe with equal firmness that the ruin of man is entirely the result of his own sin. It is the will of God that saves; it is the will of man that damns. Jerusalem stands and is preserved by the grace and favor of the Most High; but Jerusalem is burnt, and her stones are cast down, through the transgression and iniquity of men, which provoked the justice of God.

There are great deeps about these two points. The practical part of theology is that which it is most important for us to understand. Any man may get himself into a terrible labyrinth who thinks continually of the sovereignty of God alone, and he may equally get into deeps that are likely to drown him if he meditates only on the free will of man. The best thing is to take what God reveals to you and to believe that. If God's Word leads me to the right, I go there; if it leads me to the left, I go there; if it makes me stand still, I stand still. If you so act, you will be safe, but if you try to be wise above that which is written and to understand that which even angels do not comprehend, you will certainly confuse yourself. I desire ever to bring before you practical rather than mysterious subjects, and our present theme is one that concerns us all. The great destroyer of man is the will of man. I do not believe that man's free will has ever saved a soul, but man's free will has been the ruin of multitudes. "Ye would not" is still the solemn accusation of Christ against guilty men. Did He not say at another time, "And ye will not come to me, that ye might have life" (John 5:40)? The human will is desperately set against God and is the great devourer and destroyer of thousands of good intentions and emotions that never come to anything permanent because the will is acting in opposition to that which is right and true.

What God Is to Those Who Come to Him

He gathers them, "as a hen gathereth her chickens under her wings." It is a very marvelous thing that God would condescend to be compared to a hen, that the Christ, the Son of the Highest, the

Savior of men, should stoop to so basic a piece of imagery as to liken
Himself to a hen. There must be something very instructive in this
metaphor or our Lord would not have used it in such a connection.

If you have been gathered to Christ, you know first that *by this
wonderful Gatherer, you have been gathered into happy associations.* The
chicks, beneath the wings of the hen, look very happy all crowded
together. What a sweet little family party they are! How they hide
themselves away in great contentment and chirp their little note of
joy! Unbelievers find very noisy fellowship, I am afraid, in this
world, but they do not get much companionship that helps them,
blesses them, or gives them rest of mind. But if you are gathered to
the Lord's Christ, you have found there are many sweetnesses in
this life in being beneath the wings of the Most High. He who
comes to Christ finds father and mother and sister and brother; he
finds many dear and kind friends who are themselves connected
with Christ, and who therefore love those who are joined to Him.
Among the greatest happinesses of my life, certainly, I put down
Christian fellowship. If you come to Christ and join the church that
is gathered beneath His wings, you will soon find happy fellowship! I remember that in times of persecution, one of the saints said
that he had lost his father and his mother by being driven away
from his homeland, but he said, "I have found a hundred fathers
and a hundred mothers, for into whatever Christian house I have
gone, I have been looked upon with so much kindness by those
who have received me as an exile from my native land that every
one has seemed to be a father and a mother to me." If you come to
Christ, I feel persuaded that He will introduce you to many people
who will give you happy fellowship.

But that is merely the beginning. A hen is to her little chicks,
next, a cover of safety. There is a hawk in the sky; the mother bird
can see it, though the chicks cannot. She gives her peculiar cluck of
warning, and quickly they come and hide beneath her wings. The
hawk will not hurt them now; beneath her wings they are secure.
This is what God is to those who come to Him by Jesus Christ: *He
is the Giver of safety.* "He shall cover thee with his feathers, and
under his wings shall thou trust: his truth shall be thy shield and
buckler" (Ps. 91:4). You shall be preserved from all these perils—
even the attraction of your old sins or the danger of future
temptations—when you come to Christ and thus hide under Him.

The figure our Lord used is full of meaning, for in the next place, the hen is to her chicks *the source of comfort*. It is a cold night, and they would be frozen if they remained outside. But the hen calls them in, and when they are under her wings, they derive warmth from their mother's breast. It is wonderful, the care of a hen for her little ones. She will sit so carefully and keep her wings so widely spread that they may all be housed. What a cabin, what a palace it is for the young chicks to get there under the mother's wings! The snow may fall or the rain come pelting down, but the wings of the hen protect the chicks. If you come to Christ, you shall have not only safety but also comfort. I speak what I have experienced. There is a deep, sweet comfort about hiding yourself away in God, for when troubles come wave upon wave, blessed is the man who has a God to give him mercy upon mercy. When affliction or bereavement comes, when loss of property comes, when sickness comes in your own body, there is nothing wanted but your God. Apart from Him, ten thousand things cannot satisfy you or give you comfort. There, let them all go; but if God is yours and you hide away under His wings, you are as happy in Him as the chicks are beneath the hen.

The hen is also to her chicks *the fountain of love*. She loves them; did you ever see a hen fight for her chicks? She is a timid enough creature at any other time, but there is no timidity when her chicks are in danger. What an affection she has for them; not for all chicks, for I have known her to kill the chickens of another brood; but for her own what love she has! Her heart is all devoted to them. But, oh, if you want to know the true fountain of love, you must come to Christ! You will never have to say, "Nobody loves me." The love of Jesus fills to overflowing the heart of man and makes him content under all circumstances. Be reconciled to God and gathered to His blessed name.

The hen is also to her chicks *the cherisher of growth*. They would not develop if they were not taken care of. In their weakness, they need to be cherished, that they may come to the fullness of their perfection. And when the child of God lives near to Christ and hides beneath His wings, how fast he grows! There is no advancing from grace to grace, from feeble faith to strong faith, and from little fervency to great fervency, except by getting near to God.

The emblem used by our Lord is far more instructive than I have space to explain. When the Lord gathers sinners to Himself, then it is that they find in Him all that the chicks find in the hen, and infinitely more.

What God Does to Gather Men

They are straying and wandering about, but God gathers them. According to the text, Jesus says, "How often would I have gathered thy children together!" How did God gather those of us who have come to Him?

He gathers us first *by making Himself known to us.* When we come to understand who He is and what He is and know something of His love and tenderness and greatness, then we come to Him. Ignorance keeps us away from Him, but to know God and His Son, Jesus Christ, is eternal life. So I urge you to diligently study the Scriptures and to faithfully be listening to a biblical preacher of the gospel so that, knowing the Lord, you may by that knowledge be drawn toward Him. These are the cords of love with which the Spirit of God draws men to Christ. He makes Christ known to us; He shows us Christ in the grandeur of His divine and human nature, Christ in the humiliation of His sufferings, Christ in the glory of His resurrection, Christ in the love of His heart, in the power of His arm, in the efficacy of His plea, in the virtue of His blood. And as we learn these sacred lessons, we say, "That is the Christ for me; that is the God for me," and thus we are gathered to Christ.

But God gathers many to Himself *by the calls of His servants.* You see that in the Old Testament He sent His prophets; today He sends His ministers. If God does not send us to you, we shall never gather you. If we come to you in our own name, we shall come in vain. But if the Lord has sent us, He will bless us, and our message will be made as a means of gathering you to Christ. I would much rather cease to preach than be allowed to go on preaching but never to gather souls to God. I can truly say that I have no wish to say a pretty thing or utter a nice figure of speech. I want to win your souls, to slay your sin, to do practical work for God, with every reader. It is thus that God gathers men to Himself, by the message that He gives to them through His servants.

The Lord has also *many other ways of calling men to Himself.* You recall that Peter was called to repentance by the crowing of a cock, and the Lord can use a great many means of bringing sinners to Himself. Omnipotence has servants everywhere, and God can use every kind of agent, even though it appears most unsuitable, to gather together His own chosen ones. He has called you to come, and it puts it as a matter of wonder, "How often!" with a note of exclamation. Let me ask you how often God has called you. Conscience has whispered its message to you. When you see others dying, if you talk seriously to them, they will sometimes tell you that they are unprepared but that they have often had tremblings and suspicions, they have long suffered from unrest, and sometimes they have been "almost persuaded." They have been made to shake and tremble at the thought of the world to come. How often has it been so for you? "How often," God says, "would I have gathered you!"

The Lord sometimes speaks to us not so much by conscience as by providence. That death in the family—what a voice it was to us! When your mother died or your father passed away, what a gathering time it seemed to be then. You soon forgot all about it, but you did feel it then. Ah, my dear woman, when your child was so sick you thought you would lose her, then was the Lord going forth in His providence to gather you. You were being gathered, but you would not come.

It has not always been by death that the Lord has spoken to you, for you have had other calls. When you were brought low, or when a Christian friend has spoken to you, when you have read something that has compelled you to pull up and made you stand aghast for a while, has not all that had a reference to this text? "How often, how often, how often would I have gathered thee?" God knocks many times at some people's doors. I wish you would try to count how often the Almighty God has come to you and spread out His warm, wide wings, and yet "you would not."

One more way in which God gathers men is *by continuing still to have patience with them and sending the same message to them*. I am always afraid that those who listen to me regularly will get to feel, "We have heard him so long and so often that he cannot say anything new." Perhaps those who first heard the message from me were compelled to tears in the early days of coming to our church, but now they hear it all without a tremor. They are like the blacksmith's dog that goes to sleep while the sparks are flying from the anvil. Down in Southwark, at a place where they make huge boilers, a man has to get inside to hold the hammer while they are riveting. There is such an awful noise the first time that a man goes in that he feels he cannot stand it, but after a while, they tell me, he loses his hearing in such a terrible din, and some have been known even to go to sleep while the men have been hammering. So it is in hearing the gospel; men grow hardened, and that which was, at the first, a very powerful call seems to be, at the last, no call at all. God still speaks to you, not saying, "Go," but "Come, come." Christ has not yet said to you, "Depart, ye cursed," but He still cries, "Come unto me, all ye that labour and are heavy laden, and I will give you rest" (Matt. 11:28). This is how God calls and gathers men by the pertinacity of His infinite compassion in still inviting them to come to Him that they may obtain eternal life.

What Men Need to Make Them Come to God

According to our text, God does gather men, but what is needed on their part? Our Savior said of those who rejected Him, "Ye would not."

What is needed is, first, *the real will to come to God.* A will toward that which is good is required. There is where the sinner fails; what he needs is a real will. "Oh, yes!" men say, "we are willing, we are willing." But you are not willing. If we can get the real truth, you are not willing; there is not true willingness in your hearts, for a true willingness is *a practical willingness.* The man who is willing to come to Christ says, "I must put away my sins, I must put away my self-righteousness, and I must seek Him who alone can save me."

Men often talk about being willing to be saved and dispute about free will, but when it comes to actual practice, they are not willing. They have no heart to repent, they will to keep on with their sins, they will to continue in their self-righteousness. They do not will, with any practical resolve, to come to Christ. There is need of *an immediate will.* I have never met with a person yet who was not willing to come to Christ before he dies. But are you willing to come to Christ now? "To day if ye will hear his voice, harden not your hearts" (Heb. 3:7–8). But you answer, "My heart is not hardened. I ask only for a little more time." A little more time for what? A little more time in which to go on rebelling against God? A little more time in which to turn the awful risk of eternal destruction?

With others, it is *a settled will* that is needed. Oh yes, they are ready! They feel moved from the moment the preacher begins to speak, they are impressed during the singing of the first hymn, and they come forward at the close of the service. But look at those same people on Wednesday. They are as cold as a cucumber. Every feeling that they had on Sunday is gone, and they have no memory of it whatever. Their goodness is as the morning cloud, and as the early dew, it passes away. How some people do deceive us with their good resolves in which there is nothing at all, for there is no settled will.

Some lack *a submissive will.* Yes, they are willing to be saved, but they do not want to be saved by grace. They are not willing to give themselves totally to the Savior. They will not renounce their own righteousness and submit to the righteousness of Christ. Practically, that means that there is not any willingness at all, for unless you accept God's way of salvation, it is no use for you to talk about your will. Here is the great evil that is destroying you and will destroy you before long and land you in hell: "Ye would not, ye would not." Oh, that God's grace might come upon you, subduing and renewing your will and making you willing in the day of His power!

What Becomes of Men Who Will Not Be Gathered to Christ?

The text suggests two ways of answering the question, *What becomes of chicks that do not come to the shelter of the hen's wings?* The hawk devours some, and the cold nips others; they miss the warmth and comfort that they might have had. That is something. If there were no hereafter, I should like to be a Christian. If I had to die like an animal, the joy I find in Christ would make me wish to be His follower. You are losers in this world if you love not God; you are losers of peace, comfort, strength, and hope, even now. But what will be your loss hereafter, with no wing to cover you when the destroying angel is abroad, no feathers beneath which you may hide when dread thunderbolts of justice shall be launched, one after another, from God's right hand? You have no shelter, and consequently no safety. He who has no refuge in that day will be among the great multitude who will call to the rocks and the mountains to fall upon them to hide them from the face of Him who sits upon the throne and from the wrath of the Lamb. I pray you, run not the awful risk of attempting to live without the shelter of God in Christ Jesus!

But the text suggests a second question: *What became of Jerusalem in the end?* "O Jerusalem, Jerusalem!" The Jewish historian Josephus tells us what became of the inhabitants of that guilty city. They crucified the Lord of glory, and they hunted out His disciples, and yet they said to themselves, "We live in the city of God, no harm can come to us. We have the temple within our walls, and God will guard our holy place." But very soon they tried to overthrow the Roman yoke, and there were different sets of zealots who determined to fight against the Romans, and they murmured and complained and began to fight among themselves.

Before the Romans attacked Jerusalem, the inhabitants had begun to kill one another. The city was divided into various factions, three parties took possession of different portions of the place, and they fought against one another night and day. This is what happens to ungodly men: manhood breaks loose against itself, and when there are inward contentions—one part of man's soul fighting against another part—an internal war of the most horrible kind breaks out. What is the poor wretch to do who is at enmity with himself, one part of his nature saying, "Go," another part crying, "Go back," and yet a third part shouting, "Stop where you are"? Are there not many people who are just like battlefields trampled with the hoofs of horses, torn up into ruts made by cannon wheels, and stained with blood? Many a man's heart is just like that. "Rest?" says he. "That has gone from me long ago." Look at him in the morning after a drinking bout; look at him after he has been quarreling with everyone; look at the man who has been unfaithful to his wife, or that other man who has been dishonest to his employer, or that other who is gambling away all that he has. How does he sleep, poor wretch? He does not rest; he dreams; he is always in terror. I would not change places with him for anything. The depths of poverty and an honest conscience are immeasurably superior to the greatest luxury in the midst of sin. The man who is evidently without God begins to quarrel with himself.

Finally, one morning, those who looked over the battlements of Jerusalem cried, "The Romans are coming, indeed they are marching up toward the city." Vespasian came with an army of 80,000 men, and after a while, Titus had thrown up mounds around the city so that no one could come in or go out. He had surrounded it so completely that they were all shut in. It was at the time of the Passover, when the people had come from every part of the land, a million and more of them, all shut up in that little city. So a time comes, with guilty men, when they are shut up. This sometimes happens before they die: they are shut up, they cannot have any pleasure in sin as they used to have, and they have no hope. They have not been gathered to God's love, but now, at last, they are gathered by an avenging conscience; they are shut up in God's justice.

I shall never forget being called for, in the early days of my ministry, to see a man who was dying. As I entered the room, he greeted me with a curse. I was only seventeen at the time, and he somewhat staggered me. He would not lie down on his bed, and he defied God and said he would not die. "Shall I pray for you?" I asked. I knelt down, and I had not uttered many sentences before he cursed me in such dreadful language that I jumped to my feet. Again he cried and begged me to pray with him again, though he said, "Your prayer will never be heard for me. I am damned already." The poor wretch spoke as though he really were so and were realizing it in his own soul. I tried to persuade him to lie down upon his bed, but it was to no avail. He tramped up and down the room as fast as he could go, knowing that he should die but feeling that he could not die while he could keep on walking, and so he kept on. Then again I would pray with him, and then would come another awful burst of blasphemy, because it was not possible that the prayer should be heard. It does not often happen that one meets a person quite so bad as that, but there is a condition of heart that is not so visible but is quite as sad and comes to men dying without Christ. They are shut up. The Roman soldiers are, as it were, marching all around the city, and there is no escape, and they begin to feel it, and so they die in despair.

But then, when the Roman soldiers did come, the woes of Jerusalem did not end. There was a famine in the city, a famine so dreadful that what Moses said was fulfilled, and the tender and delicate woman ate the fruit of her own body. They came to search the houses because they thought there was food there, and a woman brought out half of her own babe and said, "Well, eat that, if you can," and throughout the city, they fed upon one another. Oh, when there is no God in the heart, what a famine it makes in a man's soul! How he longs for a something that he cannot find and that all the world cannot give him, not even a mouthful to stay the ravenousness of his spirit's hunger!

And this doom will be worse still in the next world. You know that Jerusalem was utterly destroyed; not one stone was left upon another. And this is what is to happen to you if you refuse your Savior: you will be destroyed, you will be an eternal ruin, no temple of God, but an everlasting ruin. Destroyed from the presence of God and the glory of His power, and so abiding forever, with no indwelling God, no hope, no comfort. How terrible will the doom be! I pray you, come and be gathered by your God.

I think I hear you reasoning in your hearts and whispering, "Who are we that we could feed this multitude? Look at their host. Who can even count them? As the stars of heaven, so are the seed of Adam. These hungry souls are almost as numerous as the sands on the seashore. How would we ever feed them all? Even so, remember, this is your mission. It never fares well to adopt a weakness of faith that was illustrated by Philip's questioning. If ever the world is to be fed, it is with Christ through the Church. Until the kingdoms of the world become the kingdoms of our Lord and of His Christ, we are the warriors who must carry the victorious arms of the cross to the uttermost parts of the earth. We are the providers of God's free bounty until the fullness of the Gentiles is gathered in. God commands all men everywhere to repent, and we are to declare His mandate. You are aware how Jesus worked the work of His Father; you know how He went about doing good; but do you know how He said, "Greater works than these shall he [that believ-eth] do; because I go unto my Father" (John 14:12). Let the words sink down into your heart. Let the vision rise perpetually before your eyes. See your work. Great as it is, and discouraged as you may be by the great multitude who desire your help, recognize the appeal to your faith. Let the magnitude of the mission drive you the more sincerely to the work instead of deterring you from it.

Chapter Seven

Compassion for the Multitude

And Jesus went forth, and saw a great multitude, and was moved with compassion toward them, and he healed their sick. And when it was evening, his disciples came to him, saying, This is a desert place, and the time is now past; send the multitude away, that they may go into the villages, and buy themselves victuals
—Matthew 14:14–15.

AS BELIEVERS, WE ARE CALLED by God to live as Christ lived in this world. As Jesus was "the true Light, which lighteth every man that cometh into the world" (John 1:9), so He told His disciples, "Ye are the light of the world" (Matt. 5:14). How memorable are those words of our Lord: "As thou has sent me into the world, even so have I also sent them into the world" (John 17:18). And how weighty are those expressions of the apostle Paul: "we pray you in Christ's stead" (2 Cor. 5:20) and "we then, as workers together with him" (2 Cor. 6:1).

There is something more than an interesting parallel that I want you to observe. A rich allegory appears to be couched in the simple record of the evangelists. The history of Christ is in type a history of His Church. You will remember how Christ's Church was wrapped in swaddling bands at the first, how she was laid in the manger of obscurity, how her life was conspired against by heathen kings. You will remember her baptism of the Holy Spirit, her trials and temptations in the wilderness. The life of Christ afterward will soon be thought out by you as a shadowing forth a picture of the career of the Church. There is hardly a point in the entire history of Jesus, from the manger at Bethlehem to the garden of Gethsemane, that is not a typical and pictorial history of His Church.

Thus the Lord has been pleased to give His Church a great example written in His own holy life. As He raised the dead, so is she to do it through His Spirit that dwells in her. As He healed the sick, so is she to carry on a great healing ministry throughout the world. Or, to come to our text, as Christ was moved with compassion to feed the hungry, so the Church, wherever she meets those who hunger and thirst after righteousness, is to bless them in the name of Him who has said, "They shall be filled" (Matt. 5:6). The business of the Church, and my business as a member of the Church of Christ, is to feed hungry souls who are perishing for lack of knowledge of the bread of life. The case before us furnishes a noble picture of our duty, of our mission, and of what we expect the Master to do for us that we may work mightily for Him.

This miracle is recorded by Matthew, Mark, Luke, and John. There are some differences in each, as there naturally would be, for no four spectators could give the same description of any one scene. But what one omits another supplies; a point that will be most interesting to one fails to strike another, while a third has been interested in something that the fourth had altogether omitted. It appears that Christ had sought out a wilderness region near the town of Bethsaida, a place that He had frequently visited. On another occasion, He had sternly warned Bethsaida and Chorazin, reminding them that their privileges would rise up in judgment against them to condemn them for their unbelief (Matt. 11:21–22). He had sought out this place for the sake of both Himself and His disciples, that they might rest from their weary toils.

But the people followed Him, thronging Him all day long. The sight of a vast multitude should always move us to pity, for it represents a mass of ignorance, sorrow, sin, and necessity far too great for us to estimate. The Savior looked upon the people with an omniscient eye, seeing perfectly all their sad condition. He *saw* the multitudes in an emphatic sense, and His soul was stirred within Him at the sight. His was not the transient tear of Xerxes when he thought on the death of his armed myriads, but it was practical sympathy with the hosts of mankind. No one cared for them; they were like sheep without a shepherd or like a field of wheat ready to spoil for lack of harvesters to gather the crop in. Jesus therefore hastened to the rescue. He noticed, no doubt with pleasure, the eagerness of the crowd, and though weary Himself, He rose in compassion to meet their needs. Such was always His way, and so must our way be as well.

Jesus preached to them the gospel, healed their sick; and sometime in the afternoon, ever patient and aware of human needs, the Master called Philip to Himself. Philip was from Bethsaida, and He said to him, "When shall we buy bread that these may eat?" This Jesus asked to see whether Philip's faith was proof against misgiving. Had Philip been wiser, he would have replied, "Master, You can feed them." But he was a weak follower of the mighty Lord. You know that afterward Philip proved his ignorance by saying, "Lord, shew us the Father, and it sufficeth us," and he then received a mild rebuke: "Have I been so long time with you, and yet hast thou not known me?" (John 14:8–9). On this, Philip shows that he had not yet learned the lesson of faith. He cannot believe in anything he cannot see with his eyes.

Puzzled and amazed, Philip approaches one of his fellow disciples to talk over the matter. Andrew suggests that there is a boy close by who has five barley loaves and a few small fishes. Certainly, Andrew thinks, though they will not be enough, *it is our duty to do our best.* So the loaves and fishes are purchased out of the small funds that Judas handed out, not perhaps without some grief to his heart, that he should have to look so much after other people. As the day wears on and the sun begins to set, the disciples come to the Master. Though the proposal had been suggested by Him, they seem to think He has forgotten it. So they come to Him and say, "Master, send the multitude away." They had thought over the problem of how to feed these people and had come to the conclusion that they could not do it. As they could not feed them, the next best thing would be to send them away to provide for themselves. Since they could not supply their necessities, they would endeavor to shut their eyes to their needs. "Master, send them away; let them go and buy for themselves."

The Master promptly replies, "They need not depart. There is no necessity for it. You give them to eat." Indeed, He spoke wisely. Why should hungry men depart from Him who feeds all things, who opens His hand and satisfies the desire of every living thing. "Give ye them to eat," said He, that He might bring out from the disciples a fair acknowledgment of their poverty. "Master," they said, "we have here but five barley loaves and a few small fishes. What are they among so many?" Lifting up their eyes upon the vast assembled group, they roughly calculate that there must be five thousand men, beside a fair complement of women and children. The Master bid them bring those loaves and fishes. He takes them, but before He breaks them, being a God of order, He tells the people to sit down in groups. Mark, who is always such a keen observer and paints all the finest details of the picture, says that they sat down on the green grass, as if it were exceedingly abundant verdure. Then he adds, they sat down in companies, afterward using a word that is translated "in ranks" in our version, but the Greek is such as you would use if you spoke of a long range of beds in a flower garden. They sat down in green beds, as it were, with walks in between them. Mark seems to present the idea that they were like a number of flowers whom his Master went round to water.

When they had all sat down, so that the strong might not struggle after the bread and tread it under foot and that the weak might not be neglected, all placed in their rows, the Master lifted up His eyes before them all, asked a blessing, broke the bread, and gave it to the disciples, and also gave the fishes. The disciples went round and distributed to each man, each woman, and each child, and they did eat. They had not eaten all day, so I dare say we should lay emphasis on the word, "they *did* eat." They ate till their hunger was appeased and they were filled. Then, I could suppose, on a spot of the green grass, where Christ had laid out the first bread and fishes, the fragments that lay there had in the meantime multiplied. One does not like the idea of the disciples going around to gather up the odds and ends and crumbs that had fallen from each person; one would hardly think it would have been appropriate. But here was bread that was not damaged, that had not fallen in the dust or the mire—fragments, and they gathered up far more than they had had at the beginning.

Here, too, we have a wonder. Things had been multiplied by division and had been added to by subtraction. More was left than there had been at the first. No doubt that was done to disarm doubt and defeat skepticism. In later days, some of those men might say, "True, we ate and were satsified, or it seemed like we did, but it might have been in a kind of dream." That bread that was left, the twelve baskets full, furnished something solid for them to look at so that they might not think it an illusion. They gathered up the twelve baskets full. This seems to be the crowning part of the miracle. Our Lord Himself, in referring to the miracle in later days, constantly says, "When we fed five thousand with five barley loaves, how many baskets had ye? And when we fed four thousand, how many baskets full did ye take up?" as if the taking up of the baskets full at the end was the clenching of the nail to drive home the blessed argument that Jesus is the Christ, the Son of God who gave His people bread to eat, even as Moses fed the Israelites with manna in the wilderness.

From our Lord's compassion for the multitude we gather two practical lessons. The text and the miracle itself teach us, first, *our mission and our weakness*, and second, *our line of duty and Christ's strength*.

Our Mission and Our Weakness

Our mission! Behold before you this very day, thousands of men and women and children who are hungering for the bread of life. They hunger till they faint. They spend their money for that which is not bread and their labor for what does not satisfy. They fall down famished in your streets, perishing for lack of knowledge (Hos. 4:6). Still worse, when they faint, there are some who pretend to feed them. Superstition goes about and offers them stones instead of bread, and serpents instead of fish. Religionists and ceremonialists offer to sell these hungry souls something to gratify them; they try to feed, but it will not satisfy; they do but eat the wind and swallow the whirlwind. The skeptic tries to persuade them that they are not hungry, they are only a little anxious; thus he mocks their appetite. But the soul will never be satisfied with the delusions and inventions of men. They faint; they famish; they are ready to die. Those who pretend to supply them do but mock and tantalize their needs. Nor can they feed themselves; their wallets are empty.

When Adam fell, he bankrupted all his posterity; neither man nor woman nor child among them is able to satisfy his or her own hunger. The ten thousands of the human race around the world— not one among them, should they all subscribe together, could find so much as one loaf upon which a single soul might feed. Barrenness, leanness, and sterility have seized upon all the fields of man's cultivation. They yield him nothing. Man sows, but he does not reap; he plows, but he obtains no harvest. By the works of the flesh no man living can be justified, and in the devices of human tradition or human reason, no souls can possibly find substantial comfort. As a disciple of Christ, see the great need that is before your eyes. Open the eyes of your understanding now, let your heart be moved, let your soul be moved with sympathy and pity—do feel for those millions as your Master feels! I beseech you, if you cannot help them, weep over them; let there be now before your mind's eye a clear and distinct recognition of the many hundreds and thousands who are crying to you, "Feed us, for we famish; give us bread to eat, or we die."

I think I hear you reasoning in your hearts and whispering, "Who are we that we could feed this multitude? Look at their host. Who can even count them? As the stars of heaven, so are the seed of Adam. These hungry souls are almost as numerous as the sands on the seashore. How would we ever feed them all? Even so, remember, this is your mission. It never fares well to adopt a weakness of faith that was illustrated by Philip's questioning. If ever the world is to be fed, it is with Christ through the Church. Until the kingdoms of the world become the kingdoms of our Lord and of His Christ, we are the warriors who must carry the victorious arms of the cross to the uttermost parts of the earth. We are the providers of God's free bounty until the fullness of the Gentiles is gathered in. God commands all men everywhere to repent, and we are to declare His mandate. You are aware how Jesus worked the work of His Father; you know how He went about doing good; but do you know how He said, "Greater works than these shall he [that believeth] do; because I go unto my Father" (John 14:12). Let the words sink down into your heart. Let the vision rise perpetually before your eyes. See your work. Great as it is, and discouraged as you may be by the great multitude who desire your help, recognize the appeal to your faith. Let the magnitude of the mission drive you the more sincerely to the work instead of deterring you from it.

Do I hear you say, "The multitudes are great, but the supplies are low. We have only five loaves, and they are made from barley; we have only two fishes, and they are small. There isn't enough food even for our own needs. What are these among so many?" "You tell us that we as a Church are to feed the world, but how can that be? How few are our talents! We have no wealth with which to supply our missionaries, that we may send them out by hosts to lift up the banner of Christ. There are few among us who are educated, wise, or eloquent. We feel it in our hearts, but we do not feel enough." Some of you add, "What can I do individually? Of what use can I be? And what can a few friends who are sincere do? Why, the world will laugh at such a feeble body of people. We have a mountain before us, and we have to level it to a plain. How can we do it? Our strength is not sufficient; we are lacking in power. Oh, had we the great and noble on our side! Had we kings and queens to lead us forward! Had we the rich to give their lavish treasure, the educated to give their wit, and the eloquent to give their golden speech, then we *might* succeed! But alas! Silver and gold have we none, and at the Master's feet we can lay but little as the world and the whole creation groans under its heavy load."

Then I think I hear you sigh and say again, "There is no more that we know of, no more bread to buy; we cannot buy for all this multitude." If we have little gifts ourselves, we cannot buy the eloquence of others. Indeed, it is no use if it were bought, for *oratory* purchased is of no use to any cause. We need for Christ's cause the free utterance of willing men who speak from their hearts what they propound with their lips. Such speak because they cannot help speaking. "Woe is unto me, if I preach not the gospel!" (1 Cor. 9:16). If we have little ability of our own, we cannot buy more from others. The offices of love can never be purchased. But I think I hear your disheartened spirits crying, "If we could add mercenary troops to the host of God, we might succeed. If we could add more strength in numbers for the host of God by donations of money, we might have enough bread in His house to feed the multitude." But millions of dollars would not suffice for the thousands of millions of needy people in the world. What can we possibly do for them?

And then I hear the groan of one who is growing gray in years. "Oh, I feel it, but it is too late for me, and the needs of the world are too weighty. The night is coming toward a sin-weary world, a long, dreary night, but we are weak and ready to go down into our graves ourselves." Let me tell you, we who are in our youth, we feel that, too. Our days spin around us now, and our weeks seem to be hissing through the air, leaving a track like that of a burning brand. Work as we may, and some of us can say that we never waste a minute in Christ's cause, yet we can do nothing. We feel like one man alone against an innumerable host, or like a child seeking to remove a mountain with its own small hand. Night comes, we are growing old, our years are flying by, our deaths are coming on. Souls are dying; hell is filling. Down the rapids of destruction men are being plunged incessantly beyond our sight, beyond our hope. We cannot do it. The more we feel our responsibility, the more our weaknesses oppress us. We have been called to a work that is too hard. We cannot do it, Master. We come to Your feet, and we confess that we cannot give these multitudes the food they need. Do not command us to impossibilities. You have commanded us to preach the gospel to every creature under heaven. We cannot reach them. We are too few, we are too weak, we are too lacking in talent. Master, we cannot do it. At Your feet we are ready to fall in sheer despair.

But listen again! I hear the cries of the multitudes as they arise. They say to us, "We are perishing; will you let us perish? We are starving; will you let us starve? Our fathers have gone down to hell, and our fathers' fathers have perished for lack of the bread that came down from heaven, and will you let us die?" Across from Africa the multitudes look over the sea to us, and they beckon: "Will you let us perish in our animism and Islamic cultures?" From Asia they lift up the cry: "Will you always leave us? Shall we always be the bondslaves of Brahman, Sheva, and Vishnu?" From Australia the Aborigines cry to us, such as have not already perished: "Shall we never see the light?" Yet the same cry is heard in our own city streets. Oh, how terrible is the wail that comes up from all the nations under heaven!

One man in Paul's dream, who said, "Come over into Macedonia, and help us" (Acts 16:9) was enough to constrain him; and here are millions, not in a dream but in open vision, who all at once say, "Come and help us." Did we say just now we could not? Surely we recall our words and say we must. Good Master, we must! If we cannot, we must. We feel our weakness, but there is an impulse within us that says we must do it, and we cannot stop; we dare not. The blasts of hell and the wrath of heaven would fall upon us if we renounced the task. The world's only hope—shall we put that out? The lone star that gilds the darkness—shall we quench that? The saviors of men, and shall we fold our arms and let them die? No! By Your love we bear Your name. By the bonds that unite us to You, by everything that is holy before God and humane in the sight of our fellow mortals, by everything that is tender and gentle in the throbbing of our hearts and the yearning of our souls, we say we must, though we feel we cannot.

Still, there is a strong tendency in our hearts to shift personal responsibility. "Let us send them away into the villages to buy meat." We look toward Bethsaida in the distance and say, "We share this task with all those we are around. There are other churches. Let them do their part. There are other Christian workers to take care of part of the multitude. Let the people go into the villages and get meat." Ah, but not so! The Master said to you, "Give *ye* them to eat." May our own church feel that it should look upon the world as if it were the only church and do its utmost as if it had no helper under heaven but had all the work to do itself. And let the entire body of the Church of our Lord Jesus Christ—instead of looking to mission groups for evangelization or to business or to governments—remember that she is the sole savior of the world. Christ never was incarnate in kings and princes. His incarnation today is in the host of His elect. If you ask me where was God on earth, I point to the man Christ Jesus. If you ask me where is Christ on earth, I point you to His faithful Church, called by His Spirit. As Christ was the world's hope, so is the Church the world's hope, and she must take up the charge as if there were no other. Instead of sending some to this town and some to that, she must hear her Master say, "Give ye them to eat."

I fear that many of us get into a careless state about perishing men, because we keep out of their way. To stop your ears to the cries of the hungry or shut your eyes to the needs of the widow and the fatherless is not the way to relieve famine. Nor is it the way of doing good in the world to avoid the haunts of the poor and to leave the dens of desolation and sin. It is ours to touch the leper with our healing finger, not to shrink from his presence. It is ours to go and find the beaten and wounded and helpless and then to pour in the oil and the wine. Leave the priest and the Levite, if they will, to pass by on the other side. Your Master asks of you practical, personal service, and your Christianity is worth nothing unless it makes you heed His word: "Give ye them to eat"—unless it makes you as individual members and as a united body to do God's work for the world's sake and for Jesus Christ's sake. I will tell you, the people of God, that the world's salvation is given instrumentally into your hands. As far as your power lies, you are to consider yourselves as the world's hope, and you are to act as such. And what shall I say if, instead of accepting this charge from Christ, you sit still and do nothing? If, after having built your own church building, you should disregard others who hear not the Word of Christ—if, being fed with heaven's food yourselves, you are satisfied to let others perish, I tell you that as a church, Ichabod is written upon your forehead. The garments of the church shall be rent, and her veil shall be torn away from her. She shall be set as a hissing; she shall be made a pillar of salt, like Lot's wife, throughout all generations if she dare look back now that the Master has called her to a great and solemn work. He who puts his hand on the plow and looks back is not worthy of the kingdom. I have faith that you will not turn back but will accept the awful charge that devolves upon you of giving light to the world. But if you reject it, I will be a swift witness against you at the last great day, that you knew your Master's service and yet sat back with indolence and sloth.

Our Duty and the Master's Strength

Our line of duty begins, first of all, in immediate obedience to Christ's first command: "Bring them to Me." "But five loaves are all we have, and two fishes." "Bring them to Me." In Mark, the words used are "go and see." They were to look in their wallets and be quite sure that they had no more. They were to rummage among all their treasures and bring out every crust, every piece of meat or bread to Christ. No matter what is found, the Master says, "Bring them to Me." The Church's first duty is, when she looks to her resources and feels them to be utterly insufficient for her work, still to bring all that she has to Christ.

But how shall she bring them? Why, in many ways. She must bring them to Christ *in consecration*. There is a brother over there who says, "I have only a little money to spare." "Never mind," says Christ, "let what you have be brought to Me." "But I have very little time to give beyond my daily work," another says. "Bring it to Me." Someone else pleads, "You don't seem to realize how small my talents are. I am not educated, and my speech is contemptible." "Bring it to Me." "I could only teach a Sunday school class." "Bring it to Me." Every talent that the Church has is to be brought to Christ in consecration. Indeed, anything that you have in this world that you do not consecrate to Christ's cause is to rob the Lord. Every true believer, when he gives himself to Christ, gives everything he has. "What, not provide for our family?" Yes, truly, but that is given to God. "Not provide for ourselves?" Yes, truly, so long as it is not covetous. Remember, it is our Master's business to provide for you. If He provides for you through your own working, you are doing your Master's work and receiving of His bounty, for it is His work to provide for you. But still there must be a thorough consecration of everything you have to Christ. Where your consecration ends, your honesty with God ends.

Bring them to Christ not only in consecration, but also in *prayer*. Our prayer meetings should be the times when the Church brings up all her barley loaves and fishes to Christ. To receive His blessing on them, we come together to the great Master. We who are weak come to be made strong; we who have no power of ourselves come to receive power from on high; and we wait in prayer as His disciples did in the upper room at Jerusalem, till the Spirit is poured out. It is marvelous how a person with one talent can sometimes do ten times more than another with ten talents, for he has ten times the grace. A soldier, after all, is not always useful according to his weapon. A fool with the most sophisticated weapon may perhaps destroy himself with it. Give a wise man but the poorest of firearms, and you shall find, with good and steady aim and bold advance, he shall do more service with his small weapons than the other with far better arms. So there are men who seem as if they might be leaders in God's house who are sluggards, doing nothing, while there are others who are but little in Israel, whom God through His grace makes to be mighty. Brethren, bring all that you have kept back and pour it into the Lord's storehouse, that His house may be full. "Prove me now herewith, saith the LORD of hosts, if I will not open you the windows of heaven, and pour you out a blessing, that there shall not be room enough to receive it" (Mal. 3:10).

Let us bring all we have to Christ, likewise in *faith*, laying it all at His feet, believing that His great power can make little provisions sufficient for mighty ends. All that the disciples could find were five loaves and two fishes for five thousand men. They were paltry to insignificance while they were in their hands, but Christ's touch ennobled them, and those little fishes became food for that vast multitude. Blessed is the man who, feeling that he has truly consecrated all to God, can say, "There is enough. I do not need more talent or finances. I would not wish to have more, for there is enough for His work. I know it is utterly insufficient in itself, but our sufficiency is of God." Do not tell me that we as a Church are too feeble to do much good. Do not tell me that Christianity in England is too weak for the evangelization of the whole world. No such thing: there is enough, there is plenty if the Master blesses it. If there were only six good men living and these six were consecrated to God, they would be enough for the world's conversion. It is not the multiplication of your means or the size of your organization or the qualifications of your leaders that God cares about—it is our consecrated people who are wholly His and only His. Let them believe that He can make them mighty, and they shall be mighty through God to the pulling down of strongholds.

I hesitate not to say that there are some pulpits that would be better empty than occupied, that there are some congregations to whom it would be far better if they had no preacher at all, for, having a minister who is not ordained of God and not speaking by faith, they content themselves with things as they are and grow listless. Were the sham taken away, they might cry out for a real ministry. God would bestow on them one taught of the Holy Spirit who would speak with a tongue of fire, with inward witness, and with spiritual energy, resting his confidence in God's promises and His Word. We should believe that there is enough means if Christ does but bless them, enough to bring in God's chosen ones.

"Bring ye them to Me." Once more, in *active service*. That which is dedicated to Christ in solemn covenant and in sincere prayer and in humble faith must be dedicated in active service. Are you *all* at work for Christ? Are you doing something for Christ? Is it possible that any believer should not be busy for the Master? Even the sick and dying can bear witness to Christ. Even those who cannot speak can demonstrate their Christianity by the way they live. The blind can still sing His praise. Is the Christian's the only name that is merely nominal? Is this a barren title? Is this a kind of cross that Christians shall take when they have done no deeds of arms, no valorous conflicts for Christ? Is the Christian only a thing and not a living reality? The Lord have mercy on us.

Let me urge you that as you bring all that you have to Christ, put your talent in *His* hand, whose hand was pierced for you. You give to Him who is your dearest friend; you give to Him who spared not the blood of His heart that He might redeem you. Do you not love Him? Is it not an honor to be permitted to show your love to so notable and noble a person? We have heard of women who have worked and all but starved themselves to bring food for their children, and as they put the precious morsels into the little ones' mouths, they felt their toil to be nothing because they were giving it to those they loved. And so with the believer—he should feel that he most blesses himself when he blesses Christ. And, indeed, when the Christian does something for Jesus, it more blesses him who gives than Him who takes.

Besides, when you give to Jesus, you are really giving to the multitude. I know some people think that when they are doing something for the church, they are pleasing the minister or the deacons. But it is not so. What interest have I in all the world but the love of poor souls—that God who reads the heart shall say, at the judgment day, there lives not one who desires more disinterestedly the salvation of this world than I do. And I trust I can speak the same for you who long to see the world brought to Christ. Look at that hungry world, and when you have bread, let those eyes that stare at you, let those who eat so abundantly thank you, and let that be sufficient recompense for what you have done. When you see the poor sinner lay hold of Christ so anxiously and yet so joyfully, when you see his gleaming eyes and the tears as they run down his cheek, you will say, I am too well paid to have done good to such a poor heart as this. Lord, it is enough, I have fed these hungry souls.

Bring your loaves and fishes to Christ instead of following Christ to get loaves and fishes. Like children who love to give gifts from their father to those in need, become a distributor for the heavenly Father. What a joy it is to take the consecrated talent and use it for the world. And then we also discover that there is more left over than we had when we began. What we have given to Christ is abundantly repaid, if not in temporal things, yet in spiritual. The fragments shall fill the baskets that are so liberally emptied. You shall find that while watering others, you are yourself watered. The joy you impart shall be mutual. To do good is to get good, and to distribute to others for Christ is the surest way of enriching oneself.

And when you have consecrated your talent to Christ and have a consciousness of your great mission, your next duty is to look up. Thank God for what you have got: look up! Say, "There is nothing in what I do; there is nothing in my prayers, my preachings, my goings, my doings, except You bless the whole. Lord, bless it!"

Then, when you have blessed, break it. Remember the multiplication never came until after the division, and the addition did not begin till the subtraction took place. So, then, begin to break, do good, and communicate. Go abroad and actively serve the Master, and when you have thus broken and have thus distributed to others, mind that you only distribute from Christ's own hand. He gives the blessing on it; then He gives back to you; afterward, you give it to the people. If I give my congregation to eat from what is my own, it will be of no use to them. But if, having gotten it in my study, I put it in the hand of Christ, and Christ hands it back to me, and I give it to them, they shall be fed to the full. This is Christ's way of blessing men. He does not give the blessing first to the world; it is to His disciples, and then the disciples to the multitude. We get in private what we distribute in public. We have access to God as His chosen favorites. We come near to Him. He gives to us; we give to others.

I began by setting before you a great and high mission. First, I made you say, "We cannot"; then I tried to make you say, "We must." And now I want to end by making you say, "We can." Yes! Christ is with us, and we can. God is for us, and we can. The Holy Spirit is in us, and we can. God the Holy Spirit calls us, Jesus Christ the Son of God cheers us, God the Father smiles upon us. We can, we must, we will. The kingdoms of this world shall become kingdoms of our Lord and of His Christ.

Jesus did not need excitement from the outside world to maintain the fires of His zeal. There was an inexhaustible fount of fire within; hence He was ardent but not noisy, intense but not clamorous. His first labors were very private. His kingdom came not with observation. He did not seek to entrap men into discipleship by methods that are commonly employed. His first disciples were urged to follow Him by John, who said, "Behold the Lamb of God, which taketh away the sin of the world" (John 1:29), and then the disciples asked Him, "Rabbi,...where dwellest thou?" (John 1:38). He gathered them one or two at a time; He did not raise an excitement and lead hundreds captive to enthusiasm. Instead of stirring the metropolitan city at once with His ministry, He went away to Nazareth and Cana, little towns among a rustic population. He went about healing the sick people and teaching; calling John and James and Peter and Andrew and Matthew, but making no very great headway, as we say; spending a whole day talking with a woman at a well, perfectly satisfied to be doing what others would call commonplace mission work. When He comes up to the feast at Jerusalem to preach, He stands there and declares the Word, but when He is opposed, He disappears and is back again in the quiet place of Galilee, still pursuing His lowly work of love.

Chapter Eight

The Gentleness of Jesus

He shall not strive, nor cry; neither shall any man hear his voice in the streets. A bruised reed shall he not break, and a smoking flax shall he not quench, till he send forth judgment unto victory. And in his name shall the Gentiles trust—Matthew 12:19–21.

EVERY SINGLE FRAGMENT of Scripture is precious. Short texts culled here and there, as subjects of meditation, are useful. At the same time, the practice of discoursing upon disconnected extracts may be carried too far, and sometimes the meaning of a passage may be entirely lost by not regarding its context. The Bible should be treated in the reading of it as any other book is treated, only with much more of reverential regard. Suppose that Milton's *Paradise Lost* were used as a textbook and that its general mode of usage were to take separate lines disconnected from the rest of the great poem and consider them as positive statements and suitable topics of meditation. It would be a dangerous experiment, and the great poet might well stir in his grave at the proposal. There are grand lines in that matchless epic that would bear the process and glow like diamonds on a regal brow, but nobody would form any worthy idea of the glory of the *Paradise Lost* by having it presented in portions, lines, and selected passages.

Such a mode of study reminds me of the Grecian student who,

when he had a house to sell, carried a brick about the streets to
show what kind of a house it was. The Bible should not be torn
limb from limb and its joints hung up like meat in the marketplace.
Beyond all other books it will bear dissection, for it is vital in every
sentence and word. Since it is a mosaic of priceless gems, you will
be enriched even if you extract a jewel here and there, but to
behold its divine beauty you must contemplate the mosaic as a
whole. No idea of the magnificent design of the entire Scriptures
can enter the human mind by reading them in detached portions,
especially if those separated passages are interpreted without reference to the whole of the writer's thoughts. Let Scripture be read
according to the rules of common sense, and that will necessitate
our reading through a book and following its train of thought.
Thus shall we be likely to arrive at the mind of the Holy Spirit. I say
this because I may disturb your understanding of the meaning of
this passage of Scripture, but do not be alarmed, for after I have
disturbed, I shall, most probably confirm it. I shall pull down to
build up again.

I will mainly concentrate on the well-known words: "A
bruised reed shall he not break, and smoking flax shall he not
quench, till he send forth judgment unto victory." We all probably
have our own opinion of the meaning of this verse. We rejoice that
the Lord Jesus will deal tenderly with the weak in grace and the
gentle in heart, and I am thankful that the text appears to express
that consoling truth. While I admit that the verse does teach us
that, does it teach us that directly and mainly? I think not. Read the
context and judge for yourself. The Pharisees endeavored to discover faults in the Lord Jesus, but they could find nothing against
Him except in reference to His disregard for their notions of the
Sabbath. They blamed His disciples for plucking ears of corn on the
Sabbath and the Lord Himself for performing a miracle of healing
on that day. Our Lord met them boldly and so utterly routed them
that one almost pities them while rejoicing over their ignominious
defeat. They were beaten outright and covered with shame.

Our Lord overwhelmed the Pharisees with five arguments,
any one of which completely swept the ground from under their
feet. For instance, that question, "What man shall there be among
you, that shall have one sheep, and if it fall into a pit on the sabbath
day, will he not lay hold on it, and lift it out? How much then is a
man better than a sheep?" (Matt. 12:11–12). Our Lord's victory was

complete and tended very much to weaken their authority, but He did not push His advantage so as to overturn the sway of these religious teachers. They were before Him as lamps so nearly blown out that nothing but a smoldering smoke remained, but He did not proceed to quench them. In argument He had proved their folly and crumpled them up till they were like so many bruised bulrushes. But there He paused; He did not pursue the conflict further but retired to Galilee, into the lone places and rural districts of the country and preached there the gospel. Lest a popular controversy and public tumult should arise, every time He wrought a miracle He told the healed one to conceal the fact so that it might be fulfilled: "A bruised reed shall he not break." And here let me ask, Do not the last words of this passage imply that the smoking flax will be quenched and the bruised reeds will be broken, when He shall "send forth judgment unto victory"? How will this be true if the passage refers to feeble saints? The first meaning looks in quite another direction and points at the Lord's enemies. Now is the season of His patience, but a day of His wrath is on the way. He forbore to overthrow His antagonists in the days of His flesh, but in the time of His second coming, He will break His foes in pieces with a rod of iron, He will dash them in pieces like potters' vessels. Now His voice is not heard in the streets, but soon that voice shall be heard by all living and shall resound through the abodes of the dead. Now He strives not for the mastery, but then shall He go forth conquering and to conquer. Today is the time of forbearance, gentleness, and meekness, and with humble reverence let us consider this.

The Savior's Forbearance

The passage wonderfully sets forth the Redeemer's gentleness, and we shall consider it first *in His own life on earth*. What a quiet, unobtrusive life was that of Him whom they called "the carpenter's son"! True, it was wonderfully energetic. There is a sense in which it must be not only admitted but also gloried in that our Lord did not strive and cry, for spiritually He fought against sin even unto agony and blood, and with thrilling eloquence and abundant tears He did cry out against evil and warn men to escape. He lifted up His voice like a trumpet and cried and spared not, so that His persuasive voice was heard in the street and throughout all the land His gospel was made known. But the passage teaches us that while others were contentious for power, clamorous for gain, and eager for notoriety, Jesus was not so. He raised no party, He fomented no strife, He sought no honor, He courted no popularity. He left the arena of this world's contests to others. His was another field of conflict. Although He was born to the acclamations of the angels, reverenced by strangers from a distant land, and foretold by seers and prophets, one marvels that He did not even in early youth shine forth as a star, but for thirty years He worked quietly in the workshop of Joseph and is there patiently occupied with "His father's business."

We catch a glimpse of Him in the temple, but, as in a moment, He vanishes again into obscurity. Had we been in His place, young men of mettle and warm blood, would we have waited thirty years and more? What hand could have held us back from the battle? Like the warhorse, we should have champed at the bit and pawed the ground, eager for conflict. Jesus was meekly quiet, neither striving nor crying nor causing His voice to be heard in the streets. When the time comes for Him to appear in public, He goes quietly to the banks of the Jordan, where John is baptizing a multitude in the river. He does not press forward and claim the Baptist's immediate attention, but He waits till all the people have been baptized, and then He tells John that He desires to be baptized by him. The deed is done, and the Holy Spirit descends upon Him in the river; but He does not come up out of the Jordan at once to plunge into the midst of conflict and preach a sermon with the fiery zeal of Peter on the day of Pentecost, neither does He at once go up to Jerusalem and proclaim Himself the Anointed of the Lord. Instead, He is led of the Spirit into the wilderness. His zeal was intense, but He had His spirit well in hand, and not a grain of self-seeking ever defiled His passion. The zeal of God's house had eaten Him up, yet He went quietly to the wilderness, and afterward to Cana and Capernaum and the remoter spots by the sea.

Jesus did not need excitement from the outside world to maintain the fires of His zeal. There was an inexhaustible fount of fire within; hence He was ardent but not noisy, intense but not clamorous. His first labors were very private. His kingdom came not with observation. He did not seek to entrap men into discipleship by methods that are commonly employed. His first disciples were urged to follow Him by John, who said, "Behold the Lamb of God, which taketh away the sin of the world" (John 1:29), and then the disciples asked Him, "Rabbi,...where dwellest thou?" (John 1:38). He gathered them one or two at a time; He did not raise an excitement and lead hundreds captive to enthusiasm. Instead of stirring the metropolitan city at once with His ministry, He went away to Nazareth and Cana, little towns among a rustic population. He went about healing the sick people and teaching; calling John and James and Peter and Andrew and Matthew, but making no very great headway, as we say; spending a whole day talking with a woman at a well, perfectly satisfied to be doing what others would call commonplace mission work. When He comes up to the feast at Jerusalem to preach, He stands there and declares the Word, but when He is opposed, He disappears and is back again in the quiet place of Galilee, still pursuing His lowly work of love.

Our King came among us in meek and lowly guise, and so He continued among us. You shall not find Christ pushing His way among the politicians, crying, "I claim leadership among the sons of men." Jesus never marches at the head of an admiring mob to assert His supremacy by their aid, alarming His foes by terror of their numbers; but gently gliding through the world, seen by His light rather than heard by His sound, He was content to shun fame and avoid applause. He frequently forbade the grateful patients whom He had healed to mention His name or publish the cure; His modesty and love of quiet shrank from notoriety. It was abundantly true of Him, He did not strive or cry, neither did many hear His voice in the streets. A bruised reed He did not break, and a smoking flax He did not quench.

Jesus never became a party leader and was no demagogue. There arose many in His day who claimed to be great ones, drawing many people after them by the pretense that they were the promised deliverers and creating such a clamor that the troops of Rome were brought in to crush the revolt. Never did our Lord bid His servants fight, for His kingdom was of another order. When, for once in His life, He rode in state as a king through the streets of Jerusalem, the shouting was only that of children, who said "Hosanna" in the temple, and of a willing, peaceful company of disciples, whose only weapons were palm branches and boughs of the trees. No warhorse did He ride; He chose the lowly ass. Compared with those who clamored for place and power, He was like a dumb man all His days, though able to have awed or charmed the multitudes to do His bidding. He loved the lone mountainside better than the throng of the crowd. He could not help being popular; such a speaker as He was would attract His thousands, for "never man spake like this man" (John 7:46). And such a miracle worker as He was, how could it be but that the people would follow to witness His wonders and eat of His loaves and fishes? And such a generous spirit, so noble and so free-hearted, it was little marvel that the people would have made Him a king; but He tore away from them, even though they sought Him. He came to endure, not to enjoy; to be despised, and not to be crowned. How often did He escape the congratulating crowds? He took ship and passed over to the other side; rough waters were more to His mind than hot-blooded mobs of transient admirers, who could be bought by bread and fish. His design was not to be the idol of the populace but to break their idols and lead back their hearts to God. Hence He did not strive or cry or run in the world's race or battle in her wars.

As He shunned popularity, so He made no use of the carnal force that lay ready to His hand. No doubt the priests and scribes were sometimes afraid to oppose Him, for fear of the people, but they had no need to fear that He would shelter behind the populace. He asked neither the rich nor the strong nor the many to protect Him but felt quite secure until His hour was come. He spoke openly before them, unguarded by His friends, and with neither weapon nor armor of defense. He never appealed to human passions or egged on the people against the Roman tyrants. No sentence of His can be construed into a desire to meet force by force. One of His followers, who loved Him much, said, "Lord, wilt thou that we command fire to come down from heaven, and consume them;" but He said, "Ye know not what manner of spirit ye are of" (Luke 9:54–55). In the garden of Gethsemane, He might have summoned legions of angels to the rescue, but He agonized alone. Not a single seraph came from the throne to drive away the son of perdition or the bloodthirsty priests. No destroying angel smote the men who spat in His face; no devouring flame burned up those who scourged Him. The force of His life was the omnipotence of gentle goodness. He did not lay the weight of His little finger upon the minds of men to compel them to involuntary subjection; His conquests were such as led men in willing captivity.

Only think of what He might have done; only think of what you and I would have done if we had been in His position, having such a work to do and such opponents. Have you never felt, when you have seen the sin of this world, as if you wanted to put it down and stamp it out by force? Your indignation has been stirred within you, and you have said, "I cannot bear it." How often have I not felt, "How is it that the eternal thunderbolts lie still? Had I one hour of the Lord's power, I would sweep away the whole of this filthiness." But Christ with these same thunderbolts in His hand never used them at all. He had no curses for His foes, no blows for His enemies. The only time He did use the semblance of violence was when He took the scourge of small cords and chased the buyers and sellers out of His own Father's house, a deed in which the awe inspired by His presence appears to have been the principal instrument employed. Such was His gentleness that when He might have shaken the earth and rocked the thrones of tyrants and made every idol god totter from its bloodstained throne, He put forth no such physical power but stood still with melting heart and tearful eye, inviting sinners to come to Him, using no lash but His love, no battle-ax and weapon of war but His grace.

Has it never struck you that it was strange He should have stopped in Palestine, a little, miserable strip of country, almost too insignificant to be noticed on the map? Why did He confine Himself to Israel? Why did He not at once go down to Greece, and there at Athens meet the philosophers and convince them of His superiority? Why not march to Rome and face proud Caesar, and if He must die, die in some conspicuous place, where all the world would hear of it? Ah, no! He courted no notoriety. We are always saying, "Let us push and get to the front," but when the world's march is in the wrong way, the true leader is behind. Jesus made no desperate attempts to reach leadership but relied upon the power of the Spirit and the force of love. The power of truth would, He knew, penetrate in quiet the prepared heart. He knew that the gospel, like fire, would burn its way without noise of drum or sound of trumpet, and He was satisfied to pick out His few fishermen and His other disciples, in whom His grace should be placed like a sacred deposit, and let the work go on like the silent growing of corn in the ground, which springs up without man's knowing how.

Beyond the forbearance that surrounded Christ's whole life, the same has been true with regard to *the spread of the gospel*. The passage does not refer merely to Christ personally but refers to

Christ's entire work, and it is true still of Him: "He shall not strive, nor cry; neither shall any man hear his voice in the streets." No violence has been employed in the spread of the gospel; no carnal weapon has been lifted to promote Messiah's reign. He does not strive or cry. When Mohammed would spread his religion, he commanded his disciples to arm themselves, then go and cry aloud in every street and offer to men the alternative to become believers in the prophet or die. Mohammed's was a mighty voice that spoke with the edge of the scimitar, delighting to quench the smoking flax and break the bruised reed. But the religion of Jesus has advanced upon quite a different plan. Other forces, more mighty but not so visible, have been employed to promote the sway of Jesus. Never has He invoked the secular arm; no demand has He made upon human governments to patronize or enforce Christianity. On the contrary, wherever governments have patronized Christianity at all, either they have killed it or the infinite mercy of God alone has preserved it.

Jesus would not have the unbeliever fined or imprisoned or cut off from the rights of citizenship. He would not allow any of His disciples to lift a finger to harm the vilest blasphemer or touch one hair of an atheist's head. He would have men won to Himself by no sword but that of the Spirit and bound to Him by no bands but those of love. Never in the Church of God has a true conversion been wrought by the use of carnal means; the Lord will not so far approve of the power of the flesh. You do not find the Lord calling in the pomp and prestige of worldly men to promote His kingdom or see Him arguing with philosophers that they might sanction His teaching. I know that Christian ministers do this, and I am sorry they do. I see them taking their places in debate with the men of boastful wisdom; they claim to have achieved great mental victories there, and I will not question their claim, but spiritual triumphs I fear they will never win in this way. They have answered one set of arguments, and another set has been invented the next day; the task is endless and as fruitless as chasing the waves of the sea. This is not the way of quickening, converting, and sanctifying the souls of men. Not as a great philosopher will You conquer, O Man of Nazareth, though You are indeed the possessor of all knowledge; but as the Savior of men and the Son of God shall Your kingdom come!

The power that Christ uses for the spread of His kingdom is

exercised in conversion and is as different as possible from compulsion or clamor. Conversion is the mysterious work of the Spirit upon the soul. The great change could not be produced by the fear of imprisonment, the authority of law, the charms of bribery, the clamor of excitement, or the glitter of eloquence. Men have pretended to be converted because they hope that it might benefit their business or raise their social position, but from such conversions may God deliver us. Men have been startled into thoughtfulness by the excitement that arises out of Christian zeal, but any real spiritual benefit they may have received has come to them from another source, for the Lord is not in the wind or tempest but in the still small voice. That which is wrought by noise will subside when the quiet reigns, as the bubble dies with the wave that bore it. Hearts are won to Jesus by the silent conviction that irresistibly subdues the conscience to a sense of guilt and by the love that is displayed in the Redeemer's becoming the great substitutionary sacrifice for us, that our sins might be removed. In this way conversions happen not by displays of human zeal, wisdom, or force. "Not by might, nor by power, but by my spirit, saith the LORD" (Zech. 4:6).

Nor has Christ caused His gospel to spread by any manifestation of the terrors of His deity. If this guilty land of ours were bruised beneath the feet of a destroying angel or we ourselves were made to sit in darkness that might be felt or to find our fields devastated by devouring locusts, then we dream that our countrymen would be struck down in terror at the power of Jesus. But such is not His mode of warfare: plagues are most suited for the armory of the law than for the hospital of the gospel. Jesus might, if He pleased, send down upon the worshipers of false gods such terrible judgments that they would cry out that the rocks might fall upon them and divine justice would exonerate the deed. But this is not the way of the Son of God. With wonderful patience He sits still and bears the insults of succeeding generations. Were He not almighty, He could not restrain Himself. He allows men still to chant hymns to gods of wood and stone; He allows priests still to insult Him by pretending to manufacture the flesh and blood of His humanity; He allows men to plunder deeper and deeper into sin. And all this He does while His saints are crying daily, "O Lord, how long?" He pauses in pity, waiting to be gracious, not willing that any should perish, loath to destroy. This smoking flax of heathendom, abominable as it is in His nostrils, He will not quench, and those broken reeds of ritualistic confidence on which men rely, He will not as yet break, for He is magnifying His patience and long-suffering. The day will come when He will "send forth judgment unto victory," and men shall see that the patient Lamb is also the mighty Lion of the Tribe of Judah, and He who was omnipotent to bear offenses will also be omnipotent to recompense His foes and to ease him of his adversaries.

The same truth appears in *the experience of every unconverted man*. The person who denies the existence of his Maker is like the bruised reed that He refuses to break despite the insolence they show. Men insult God with their profanity, others say that Christ is not the Son of God and so rob Him of His greatest glory, others speak against the sacrifice of Christ on the cross, and Sauls persecute His Church with a vengeance. But, oh, how is it that He sits still with such soundings in His ears? In His forbearance we find the answer. For the space of thirty, forty, fifty, perhaps sixty or seventy years His patience may have waited for us. Oh, the mercy of the Lord! The mercy of the Lord! He will not break the bruised reed or quench the smoking flax!

One more remark should be made here. Our present view of the text proves beyond all question *His compassion for those who are weak and feeble but are of a right spirit*. We generally understand the passage to mean that wherever there is a spark of grace, Christ will not quench it, and wherever there is any brokenness of heart, Christ will not destroy it. Now, observe, that instead of denying that this is the meaning of the passage, while I do not assert that it is the first meaning, I have helped you to see how forcibly this truth may be inferred from the text, for if Christ would not quench those Pharisees and Sadducees who were so obnoxious, if He does not put down cruel kings, and if He bears with infidels and skeptics and persecutors and profane persons, how much more will He deal gently with those who are truly seeking Him but whose spiritual life is feeble, so that they are comparable to bruised reeds and smoking flax. Instead of setting aside, we have rather confirmed and brought into clearer light the meaning that is usually given to the text. O poor heart, are you seeking Jesus? Is it a poor, trembling search as yet? Are you afraid that He will reject you? Have you begun to pray, but does that prayer seem too feeble to enter the gates of heaven? Be of good courage. He who has patience with His proudest foe will not be hard and censorious to a trembling sinner. It cannot be that He who is too tender to destroy the howling beast that snarls at Him should be so severe as to slay the lamb that lies at His feet.

For those of you who have placed all your hope in Christ, it may be you are depressed because you do not grow in grace as you would wish to do, and there are times when your anxiety to be right leads you to make rigid self-examination, and then you are grieved because there does not appear to be more grace in you than fire in a dying candlewick or more true life in you than there is of strength in a bruised reed. Well, never mind. Jesus has a special care for the weak and is tender to the utmost degree toward such as need to be gently handled. Only let your faith be sincere, and if it is but as a grain of mustard seed it shall bring you into the kingdom. Though you can but look with bleared eye at the cross and scarce see it by reason of the tears of your sorrow, if you do but trust in the great sacrifice, you are saved, for Jesus is no rough taskmaster toward seeking souls, no stern judge or heartless driver of the weak. He is full of pity and compassion.

The Result of the Gentleness of Christ

"And in his name shall the Gentiles trust." What does this mean? Why, power, violence, harshness, and severity are never trusted. You cannot win men's hearts by such means. When the old Napoleon was on the rock of St. Helena, he said gloomily to one of his attendants, "My empire has passed away, because it rested upon force, but the empire of Jesus lasts still, and will last forever, because it is based upon love." What has Jesus done for His subjects but loved them better than anyone else could have, suffered for them beyond all, and conferred greater blessings upon them than all the universe besides could have bestowed? By such things has He captured their hearts. You may tempt away Christ's followers from Him when you can find them a better master or a more loving friend, but not till then. You shall win us to a new leader when you can show us one better, but you cannot even imagine one who could compare for an instant with the chief among ten thousand, the altogether lovely. We who are sinners of the Gentiles trust Him, and trust Him implicitly, because He is so divinely gentle, so omnipotently tender. Savior, no tyrant are You! You do not trample on the poor and needy or oppress the weak and trembling.

You are mercy itself, love embodied, grace incarnate; therefore do the people flock to You, and in Your name do the Gentiles trust.

The power of Jesus over men lies in the fact that He has taught them to trust Him. The firm faith of His followers consolidates His kingdom. When His word comes home to us in its own soft and gentle manner and He manifests Himself to us as He does not unto the world, and when He permits us to put our finger into the print of the nails and our hand into His side, and when He says, "You are mine, and I am yours," then we feel burning in our soul like coals of juniper, that grand enthusiasm that is the terror of the adversaries of Christ and the power of the Church. More potent than the edge of the sword is the intense love of saints. As the might of the north wind when it chases away the mists, such is the divine force of love of Jesus when it fills the heart, chasing away all lethargy and sin. When we truly trust our Lord, we feel that we can do anything for Him: impossibilities have ceased, and miracles have returned. When we trust Christ, self-sacrifice becomes a joy, and holy daring is but a natural impulse. By trust in Christ, the weakest have been made strong, feeble women have routed their persecutors, and humble men have confronted the proudest despots without fear. O Lord Jesus, the Gentiles trust in You because You are meek and lowly, and their trustful love is the strength of Your growing dominion.

The End of This Gentleness

"Till he send forth judgment unto victory." The Lord is slow to anger and gives His patience room. Yet if men will not be won by love, if even the wounds of Christ cannot tear them away from their lusts, if reason is lost upon them and they make beasts of themselves, there must come an end of it. A God of all mercy and no justice would in the long run be a dreadful calamity, just as a judge who never punished crime would be the worst possible magistrate for any nation. The very instincts of our nature make us feel that sin must be punished in due time. There must come a time when the foes of God shall not rule and error shall not dominate over men. Jesus, the friend of man, will do this in a certain sense at the death of every ungodly man and woman. With what surprise will they open their eyes in the next state and see Christ, whom they have despised, sitting upon His throne. With what unutter-able dismay have some been seized, even before they have been quite dead; while the curtain was just rising and was not fully up, they have howled with horror. But, ah, their dreadful doom! Those who denied that Jesus was God shall see Him as divine; those who persecuted His people shall see His people glorified at His side; those who opposed the truth He taught shall feel how sure that truth is and shall learn how dreadful a thing it is to neglect the great salvation and fall into the hands of the living God.

But that is not all. There is a day appointed, an hour of which no man knows, when the Lord Jesus shall descend from heaven with a shout. Yes, He who was nailed to the cross, who died and rose and ascended, leaving the last print of His feet upon Olivet, He shall descend to earth again. He shall come not to suffer but to judge, and with Him shall come His own beloved followers. Then shall the dead rise from their graves, and sea and land yield up the trophies of the grave. His word shall roll like thunder and smite like lightning: "Depart from me, ye cursed, into everlasting fire, prepared for the devil and his angels" (Matt. 25:41). The day will come when truth shall bind them in chains of fire forever and ever, and He shall sweep out of His kingdom every offensive thing. God grant that we may not be exposed to His anger when He shall be among the sons of men as a refiner's fire and like fuller's soap. Amen.

This widowed mother no doubt mourned her boy not only because he was dead but also because in him she had lost her earthly help. She must have regarded him as the staff of her age and the comfort of her loneliness. "She was a widow." I question whether anyone but a widow understands the full sorrow of that word. We may put ourselves by sympathy into the position of one who has lost her other self, the partner of her life; but the tenderest sympathy cannot fully realize the actual tearing of bereavement and the desolation of love's loss. "She was a widow"—the sentence sounds like a knell. Still, if the sun of her life was gone, there was a star shining; she had a boy, a dear boy, who promised her great comfort. Her son would, no doubt, supply her necessities and cheer her loneliness, and in him her husband would live again, and his name would remain among the living in Israel. She could lean on him as she went to the synagogue. She would have him to come home from his work in the evening and keep the little home together and cheer her hearth. Alas! That star is swallowed up in the darkness. He is dead, and today he is carried to the cemetery. It is the same spiritually with us in reference to our unconverted friends. We feel that we miss the aid and comfort that we should receive from them in our service of the living God. We did look forward to see them grow up in the fear of God and to stand side by side with us in the great warfare against evil and in holy labor for the Lord Jesus; but they cannot help us, for they are on the wrong side. We have to spend thought and prayer and effort over them that might have been used for others. Our care for the great dark world that lies all around us is very pressing, but they do not share it with us.

Chapter Nine

Compassion for the Widow

And it came to pass the day after, that he went into a city called Nain; and many of his disciples went with him, and much people. Now when he came nigh to the gate of the city, behold, there was a dead man carried out, the only son of his mother, and she was a widow: and much people of the city was with her. And when the Lord saw her, he had compassion on her, and said unto her, Weep not. And he came and touched the bier: and they that bare him stood still. And he said, Young man, I say unto thee, Arise. And he that was dead sat up, and began to speak. And he delivered him to his mother. And there came a fear on all: and they glorified God, saying, That a great prophet is risen up among us; and, That God hath visited his people—Luke 7:11–16.

Behold the overflowing, everflowing power of our Lord Jesus Christ. On the previous day, He had worked a great miracle upon the centurion's servant, and now, He raises the dead. Day after day the deeds of goodness of Christ uttered their speeches in the countryside of Judea. Did He save your friend yesterday? His fullness is the same today; if you seek Him, His love and grace will flow to you. He blesses this day, and He blesses the day after. Never is our divine Lord compelled to pause until He has replenished His resources, but strength goes out of Him forever. These thousands of years have not diminished the aboundings of His power to bless.

Behold, also, the readiness and naturalness of the outgoings of His life-giving power. Our Savior was journeying to the city of Nain, and He works miracles while on the road. It was incidentally, some would say accidentally, that He met the funeral procession; but at once He restored to life this dead young man. Our blessed Lord was not standing still, as one professionally called in. He does not seem to have come to Nain at anyone's request for the display of His love, but He was simply passing through the gate into the city for a reason that is not recorded. See how Jesus is always ready to save! He healed the woman who touched Him in the throng when He was on the road to another person's house. The mere spillings over of the Lord's cup of grace are marvelous. He gives life to the dead when He is *en route*. He scatters His mercy by the roadside, and anywhere and everywhere His paths drop fatness. No time, no place, can find Jesus unwilling or unable. When Baal is on a journey or sleeps, his deluded worshipers cannot hope for his help (1 Kings 18:27), but when Jesus journeys or sleeps, a word will find Him ready to conquer death or stop the tempest.

It is a remarkable incident, this meeting of the two processions at the gates of Nain. If someone with a fine imagination could picture it, what an opportunity he would have for developing his poetical genius! Yonder a procession descends from the city. Our spiritual eyes see death upon the pale horse coming forth from the city gate with great exultation. He has taken another captive. Upon that bier behold the spoils of the dread conqueror! Mourners by their tears confess the victory of death. Like a general riding in triumph to the Roman capital, death bears his spoils to the tomb. What shall hinder him?

Suddenly the procession is arrested by another: a company of disciples and many people are coming up the hill. We need not look at the company, but we may fix our eyes upon One who stands in the center, a Man in whom lowliness was always evident and yet majesty was never lacking. It is the living Lord, even He who only has immortality; in Him death has now met his destroyer. The battle is short and decisive; no blows are struck, for death has already done his utmost. With a finger the chariot of death is arrested; with a word the spoil is taken from the mighty, and the lawful captive is delivered. Death flies defeated from the gates of the city while Mount Tabor and Herman, which both looked down upon the scene, rejoice in the name of the Lord. This was a rehearsal upon a small scale of that which shall happen soon, when those who are in their graves shall hear the voice of the Son of God and live: then shall the last enemy be destroyed. Only let death come into contact with Him who is our life and it is compelled to relax its hold, whatever may be the spoil that it has captured. Soon shall our Lord come in His glory, and then before the gates of the New Jerusalem we shall see the miracle at the gates of Nain multiplied a myriad times.

Thus, our object would naturally conduct us to the doctrine of the resurrection of the dead, which is one of the foundation stones of our most holy faith. That grand truth I have often declared, but at this time my concern is to take the literal fact and use it for spiritual instruction. All our Lord's miracles were intended to be parables: they were intended to instruct as well as to impress. They are sermons to the eye, just as His spoken discourses were sermons to the ear. We see here how Jesus can deal with spiritual death and how He can impart spiritual life to His pleasure. Oh, that we may see this done in our lives!

The Spiritually Dead
Cause Great Grief to Their Friends

If an ungodly man is favored to have Christian relatives, he causes them much anxiety. As a natural fact, this dead young man who was being carried to his burial caused his mother's heart to burst with grief. She showed by her tears that her heart was overflowing with sorrow. The Savior said to her, "Weep not," because He saw how deeply she was troubled. Many of my dear young friends may be deeply thankful that they have friends who are grieving over them. It is a sad thing that your conduct should grieve them but is a hopeful circumstance for you that you have those around you who do grieve. If all approved of your evil ways, you would, no doubt, continue in them and go speedily to destruction. But it is a blessing that arresting voices do at least a little hinder you. Besides, it may yet be that our Lord will listen to the silent oratory of your mother's tears and bless you for her sake. See how the evangelist puts it: "When the Lord saw her, he had compassion for her, and said unto her, Weep not." And then He said to the young man, "Arise."

Many people who in some respects are amiable and hopeful, nevertheless, being spiritually dead, *are causing great sorrow to those who love them best.* It would perhaps be honest to say that they do not intend to inflict all this sorrow; indeed, they think it quite unnecessary. Yet they are a daily burden to those whom they love. A mother laments over her son's decision to no longer attend church and listen to the Word of the Lord. She had hoped that he would follow in his father's footsteps and join the people of God, but he takes quite the opposite course. Her anxiety is deepened as he forms companionships and other connections that are sadly harmful to him. She sees a growing indifference to everything that is good and an unconcealed intention to see the ungodly side of life. She fears that he will go from one sin to another until he ruins himself for this life and the next. To have an unconverted child is to carry a very great grief, and yet more so if the child is her only boy and she is a widow. To see spiritual death rampant in one so dear is a sorrow that causes many a mother to mourn in secret and pour out her soul before God. Many a Hannah has become a woman of a sorrowful spirit through her own child. How sad that he who should have made her the gladdest among women has filled her life with bitterness! Many a mother has had so to grieve over her son as almost to cry, "Would God he had never been born!"

The cause of the grief lies here: *We mourn that they should be in such a case.* In the story before us, the mother wept because her son was dead, and we sorrow because our friends are spiritually dead. There is a life infinitely higher than the life that quickens our material bodies. It is a dreadful thing to be dead to God, dead to Christ, dead to the Holy Spirit. It is sad, indeed, when a person is dead to those divine truths that are the delight and strength of our souls, dead to those holy motives that keep us from evil and spur us on to virtue, dead to those sacred joys that often bring us very near the gates of heaven. We cannot look at the dead man and feel joy in him, whoever he may be: a corpse, however beautifully dressed, is a sad sight. We cannot look upon a sinner without crying out, "Son of man, can these bones live?... Come from the four winds, O breath, and breathe upon these slain, that they may live" (Ezek. 37:3, 9). The apostle Paul spoke of one as "she that liveth in pleasure is dead while she liveth" (1 Tim. 5:6). Scores of people are dead in reference to all that is truest, noblest, and most divine, and yet in other respects they are full of life and activity. To think that they should be dead to God and yet so full of energy and delight! Marvel not that we grieve about them.

We also mourn because we lose the help and comfort that they should bring us. This widowed mother no doubt mourned her boy not only because he was dead but also because in him she had lost her earthly help. She must have regarded him as the staff of her age and the comfort of her loneliness. "She was a widow." I question whether anyone but a widow understands the full sorrow of that word. We may put ourselves by sympathy into the position of one who has lost her other self, the partner of her life; but the tenderest sympathy cannot fully realize the actual tearing of bereavement and the desolation of love's loss. "She was a widow"—the sentence sounds like a knell. Still, if the sun of her life was gone, there was a star shining; she had a boy, a dear boy, who promised her great comfort. Her son would, no doubt, supply her necessities and cheer her loneliness, and in him her husband would live again, and his name would remain among the living in Israel. She could lean on him as she went to the synagogue. She would have him to come home from his work in the evening and keep the little home together and cheer her hearth. Alas! That star is swallowed up in the darkness. He is dead, and today he is carried to the cemetery. It is the same spiritually with us in reference to our unconverted friends. We feel that we miss the aid and comfort that we should receive from them in our service of the living God. We did look forward to see them grow up in the fear of God and to stand side by side with us in the great warfare against evil and in holy labor for the Lord Jesus; but they cannot help us, for they are on the wrong side. We have to spend thought and prayer and effort over them that might have been used for others. Our care for the great dark world that lies all around us is very pressing, but they do not share it with us.

A further grief is that we can have no fellowship with them. The widow of Nain could never speak to her son again. And we have dear ones whom we love and who love us, but we cannot hold any spiritual communion with them, nor them with us. They never bow the knee together with us in private prayer or mingle their heart with ours in appeal to God as to the cares that prowl around our home. O young man, when your mother's heart leaps for joy because of the love of Christ shed abroad in her soul, you cannot understand her joy. Her feelings are a mystery to you. If you are a dutiful son, you do not say anything disrespectful about her faith, but you cannot sympathize in its sorrows or joys. Between you and your mother there is upon the best things a gulf as wide as if you were actually dead on the bier and she stood weeping over your corpse. I remember the overwhelming hour when I feared that my beloved wife was about to be taken from me, how I was comforted by the loving prayers of my two dear sons. We had communion not only in our grief but also in our confidence in the living God. We knelt together and poured out our hearts to God, and we were comforted. How I blessed God that I had in my children such sweet support! But suppose they had been ungodly young men! I should have looked in vain for fellowship and for aid at the throne of grace.

Moreover, *spiritual death soon produces manifest causes for sorrow.* In the narrative before us, the time had come when the woman's son's body must be buried. She could not wish to have that dead form longer in the home with her. It is a token to us of the terrible power of death, that it conquers love with regard to the body. Abraham loved his Sarah, but after her death he quickly found a burying place for her remains. It happens in some dreadful cases where a person becomes so bad that no comfort in life can be enjoyed while the erring one is within the home. We have known parents who have felt that they could not have their son at home, so drunken, so debauched had he become. I have known mothers who could not think of their daughters without feeling pangs far more bitter than those they endured at their birth. Woe, woe to him who causes such heartbreak! What an awful thing it is when love's best hopes gradually die down into despair, and loving desires at last put on mourning and turn from prayers of hope to tears of regret! Words of admonition call forth such passion and blasphemy that prudence almost silences them. Then have we before us the dead young man carried on the bier. O young person, never allow your heart to be so turned to stone. Contemplate your parents' heartbreak and be broken yourself.

We also mourn because of the future of men dead in sin. This mother, whose son had already gone so far in death that he must be buried out of sight, had the further knowledge that something worse would befall him in the sepulcher to which he was being carried. It is impossible for her to think calmly of the corruption that surely follows at the heels of death. When we think of what will become of those who refuse the Lord Jesus Christ, we are appalled. "It is appointed unto men once to die, but after this the judgment" (Heb. 9:27). We dare not linger at the dreadful mouth of hell, but we are forced to say that there is a place where those must abide who are driven from the presence of the Lord and from the glory of His power. It is an unendurable thought to be "cast into the lake of fire. This is the second death" (Rev. 20:14). I do not wonder that those who are not honest with you are afraid to tell you so, but with the Bible in your hand and a conscience in your bosom, you cannot but fear the worst if you remain apart from Jesus and the life He freely gives. If you continue as you are, persevering in your sin and unbelief to the end of life, there is no help for it but that you must be condemned in the day of judgment. The most solemn declarations of the Word of God assure you that "he that believeth not shall be damned" (Mark 16:16). Will you take your part and lot with accursed ones, or will you come to the Lord Jesus and follow Him to glory?

Oh, that I had the forceful utterance of an Isaiah or the passionate lamentations of a Jeremiah with which to arouse your affections and your fears! Still, the Holy Spirit can use even me, and I beseech Him to do so. It is enough. I am sure you see that the spiritually dead cause great grief to those of their family who are spiritually alive.

For Such Grief There Is Only One Helper

The young man is taken out to be buried, but *our Lord Jesus Christ met the funeral procession.* The Savior that day had traveled twenty-five miles to arrive at Nain in the evening. How remarkable that His arrival was timed precisely when the young man was being hastened to his grave. See, He ascends the hill of the little city at the exact moment when the procession is coming out of the gate! He meets the dead man before the place of the sepulcher is reached. A little later and the young man would have been buried; a little earlier and he would have been lying in the darkened room at home. The Lord knows how to arrange all things; His forecasts are true to the tick of the clock. Jesus comes to you as well to meet you and quicken newness of life in you. There is no chance about it, eternal decrees have arranged it all, and we shall soon see that it is so.

The blessed Savior saw all at a glance. Out of the procession He singled out the chief mourner and read her inmost heart. He was always tender to mothers. He fixed His eye on that widow, for He knew that she was such without being informed of the fact. The dead man is her only son. Jesus perceives all the details and feels them all intensely. Jesus knows all about you. Nothing is hid from His infinite mind. Your mother's heart and yours are both open to Him. Jesus, who is invisibly present, fixes His eyes on you at this moment. He has seen the tears of those who have wept for you. He sees that some of them despair of you and are in their great grief acting like mourners at your funeral.

Jesus saw it all and, what was more, *entered into it all*. Oh, how we should love our Lord that He takes such notice of our griefs, and especially our spiritual griefs about the souls of others! You, dear teacher, want your class saved; Jesus sympathizes with you. You, dear friend, have been very sincere to win others to faith. Jesus knows all about our travail in soul, and He is at one with us. Our travail is only His own travail rehearsed in us according to our humble measure. When Jesus enters into our work, our work cannot fail. Enter, O Lord, into my work at this moment and bless the truth in these feeble words!

Our Lord proved how He entered into the sorrowful state of things by first saying to the widow, "Weep not." At this moment He says to you who are praying and agonizing for souls, "Do not despair! Sorrow not as those who are without hope! I mean to bless you. You shall yet rejoice over life given to the dead." Let us take heart and dismiss all unbelieving fear.

Our Lord went to the bier and just laid His finger upon it, and *those who bare it stood still of their own accord*. Our Lord has a way of making bearers stand still without a word. Perhaps today a young man is being carried further into sin by the bearers of his natural passions, his infidelity, his bad company, and his love of strong drink. It may be that pleasure and pride, willfulness and wickedness are bearing the four corners of the bier. But our Lord can, by His mysterious power, make the bearers stand still. Evil influences have become powerless, the man knows not how.

When they stood quite still, *there was a hush*. The disciples stood around the Lord, the mourners surrounded the widow, and the two crowds faced each other. There was a little space, and Jesus and the dead man were in the center. The widow pushed away her veil and, gazing through her tears, wondered what was coming. The Jews who came out of the city halted as the bearers had done. Hush! Hush! What will He do? In that deep silence the Lord heard the unspoken prayers of that widow. I doubt not that her soul began to whisper, half in hope and half in fear: "Oh, that He would raise my son!" At any rate, Jesus heard the flutter of the wings of desire if not faith. Surely her eyes were speaking as she gazed on Jesus, who had so suddenly appeared. Here let us be as quiet as the scene before us. Let us be hushed for a minute and pray God to raise dead souls at this time.

Jesus Is Able to Work the Miracle of Life Giving

That hush was not long, for speedily the Great Quickener entered upon His gracious work. Jesus Christ has life in Himself, and He gives life to whom He will (John 5:21). Such life is there in Him that "he that believeth in me, though he were dead, yet shall he live" (John 11:25). Our blessed Lord immediately went up to the bier. What lay before Him? It was a corpse. *He could derive no aid from that lifeless form.* The spectators were sure that he was dead, for they were carrying him out to bury him. No deception was possible, for his own mother believed him dead, and you may be sure that if there had been a spark of life in him she would not have given him up to the jaws of the grave. There was then no hope—no hope from the dead man, no hope from any anyone in the crowd either of bearers or of disciples. They were all alike powerless.

There is no help beneath the skies for anyone who is dead in his sins. No help in yourself or in those who love you best. But, lo, the Lord has laid help on One who is mighty. If Jesus wants the least help, you cannot render it, for you are dead in sins. There you lie, dead on the bier, and nothing but the sovereign power of divine omnipotence can put heavenly life into you. Your help must come from above.

While the bier stood still, Jesus spoke to the dead young man, *spoke to him personally:* "Young man, I say unto thee, Arise." O Master, personally speak to us. If You will speak to us, we shall live. "Arise!" *Jesus spoke as if the man had been alive.* This is the gospel way. He did not wait until He saw signs of life before He told him to rise, but to the dead man He said, "Arise." This is the model of gospel preaching: in the name of the Lord Jesus, His commissioned servants speak to the dead as if they were alive. We read, "Arise from the dead, and Christ shall give thee light" (Eph. 5:14). We are to tell men to believe on the Lord Jesus Christ, even though we know that they are dead in sin, and that faith is the work of the Holy Spirit. Our faith enables us in God's name to command dead men to live, and they do live. We bid unbelieving men to believe in Jesus, and power goes with the Word, and God's elect do believe. It is by this word of faith that we preach that the voice of Jesus sounds out to men. The young man who could not rise, for he was dead, nevertheless did rise when Jesus commanded him. Even so, when the Lord speaks by His servants, the gospel command "Believe and live" is obeyed, and men live.

But the Savior, you observe, *spoke with His own authority*: "Young man, *I say unto thee*, Arise." Neither Elijah nor Elisha could have spoken this way, but He who spoke thus was very God of very God. Though veiled in human flesh and clothed in lowliness, He was that same God who said, "Let there be light: and there was light" (Gen. 1:3). If any of us are able by faith to say, "Young man, arise," we can say it only in *His* name—we have no authority but what we derive from *Him*. Young man, the voice of Jesus can do what your mother cannot. How often has her sweet voice wooed you to come to Jesus but called you in vain? Oh, that the Lord Jesus would inwardly speak to you! Oh, that He would say, "Young man, arise." Perhaps the Lord is silently speaking in your heart by His Holy Spirit right now. If so, within you a gentle movement of the Spirit is inclining you to repent and yield your heart to Jesus. Do it now!

The miracle was accomplished immediately. This young man, to the astonishment of all about him, sat up. His was a desperate case, but death was conquered. He had been called back from the innermost dungeon of death, even from the grave's mouth, but he sat up when Jesus called him. It did not take a month or a week or an hour, not even five minutes. In an instant the Lord can save a sinner. Before the word I write has more than entered your eye, the divine flash that gives you eternal life can have penetrated your heart, and you shall be a new creature in Jesus Christ, no more to feel spiritually dead or to return to your old corruption. New life, new feeling, new love, new hopes, new company shall be yours because you have passed from death to life.

This Miracle Will Cause Very Great Results

The great result was manifest, first in the young man. Would you like to see him as he was? Draw back the sheet from his face and see a pallor over it. How sunken are the eyes! Come, look into this grave, where corruption has gone further in its work. Cover him up! We cannot bear the sight. But when Jesus Christ has said,

"Arise," what a change takes place! Now you may look at him. His eye has the light of heaven in it; his lips are coral with life; his brow is fair and full of thought. Look at his healthy complexion, in which the rose and the lily sweetly contend for mastery. What a fresh look there is about him, as of the dew of the morning! He has been dead, but he lives, and no trace of death is on him. And then he begins to speak! What music for his mother's ear! What did he say? Surely, I cannot tell you. But any words proved him to be alive.

If you know the Lord, I believe you will speak of heavenly things. I do not believe that our Lord Jesus has a speechless child in His house: they all speak *to* Him, and most of them speak *of* Him. The new birth reveals itself in confession of Christ and praise of Christ. The widow was just overjoyed that he spoke at all. Newly saved souls often talk in a manner that later years and experience will not justify. But if genuine grace is in their souls and they bear witness to the Lord Jesus, I for one would not criticize them. Be glad if you can see any proof that they are born again, and mark well their future lives. To the young man himself a new life had begun—life from among the dead.

A new life also had begun in reference to *his mother*. What a great result for her was the raising of her dead son! Henceforth her son would be doubly dear. Jesus helped him down from the bier and delivered him to his mother. We have not the words He used, but we are sure that He made the presentation most gracefully, giving back the son to the mother as one presents a fine gift. With a majestic delight that always goes with His condescending benevolence, He looked on that happy woman, and His glance was brighter to her than the light of the morning as He said to her, "Receive thy son." The thrill of her heart was such as she would never forget. Observe carefully that our Lord, when He puts the new life into young men, does not want to take them away with Him from the home where their first duty lies. Here and there one is called away to be an apostle or a missionary, but usually our Lord wants them to go home to their friends and bless their parents and make their families happy and holy. He does not present the young man to the priest, but He delivers him to his mother. God sends us home to charm our father and mother, to be a blessing to our brothers and sisters, and to let them rejoice that he "was dead, and is alive again"(Luke 15:24, 32).

What was the next result? Well, all the neighbors feared and glorified God. If the young man who has led a wild life is suddenly born again, all around him will wonder at it. If that young man has got himself out of wrongdoing and is saved, we shall all feel that God is very near us. If that young man who had run with evil women and had fallen into other evils is brought to be pure-minded and gracious, it will strike awe into those around him. Conversions are miracles that never cease. These prodigies of power in the moral world are quite as remarkable as prodigies in the material world. We want conversion, so practical, so real, so divine, that those who doubt will not be able to doubt because they see in them the hand of God.

Finally, note not only that it surprised the neighbors and impressed them but also that the rumor of it went everywhere. Who can tell? The result of any conversion may be felt for thousands of years, even into eternity. When you go home and tell what God has done for your soul, there will be a wide circle in influence. And if you should be called to preach the gospel, no one can tell how wide the circle will become. Ring upon ring will the word spread itself until the shoreless ocean of eternity shall feel the influence of this word. Grace this day bestowed by the Lord upon one single soul may affect the whole of humanity. According to your faith, so shall it be.

Moreover, it is a wonderful fact that He was tempted of the devil. He in whom all evil is personified dared to stand foot to foot in single duel with Him in whom all goodness is concentrated. The fiend infernal dared to face the God incarnate. God in our mortal flesh encountered the devil in the wilderness of temptation. How could the fiend have ventured to assail our Lord? Truly Lucifer was lifted up to the extreme of pride when he dared to confront his Lord. But Christ was tempted of the devil early in His public career, and again near its close, He exclaimed, "But this is your hour, and the power of darkness" (Luke 22:53). He seemed to hear the dragon's wings as they beat the midnight air, and He cried, "The prince of this world cometh" (John 14:30). Calmly He added, "and hath nothing in me"; yet His heart grew chill in the hideous presence of the great adversary. It was nothing less than an agony in Gethsemane—a painful wrestling between Jesus and the powers of darkness. You who are tempted of the devil; you who are troubled by mysterious whisperings in your ear; you who, when you sing or pray, have a blasphemy suggested to you; you who even in your dreams awake with horror at the thoughts that cross your mind, be comforted, for your Lord knows all your temptation. To you, I say, you can enter into fellowship with your Lord in His being tempted of the devil; that which is incomprehensible to others is plain enough to you.

Chapter Ten

The Suffering Savior's Sympathy

For in that he himself hath suffered being tempted, he is able to succour them that are tempted—Hebrews 2:18.

WE ARE TOLD IN HEBREWS 5 that one special requisite in a high priest was that he should have compassion upon men. "For every high priest taken from among men is ordained for men in things pertaining to God, that he may offer both gifts and sacrifices for sins: Who can have compassion on the ignorant, and on them that are out of the way; for that he himself also is compassed with infirmity" (vv. 1–2). God did not choose angels to be made high priests, because, however benevolent they might be in their wishes, they could not be sympathetic. They could not understand the peculiar needs and trials of the men with whom they had to deal. Ministers who are made to be a flame of fire could hardly commune with those who confess themselves to be as dust and ashes. But the high priest was one of themselves. However dignified his office, he was still a man. He was one of whom shared all the experiences common to other men—bereavement, sicknesses, sufferings, joys, abundances, shortages. All this was necessary that he might be able to enter into their feelings and represent those feelings before God and that he might, when speaking

141

to God, speak not as a superior but as one who sat by their side, bone of their bone and flesh of their flesh.

Now this is peculiarly so in the case of our Lord Jesus Christ. He is sympathetic above all. There is none so tender as He. He has learned it by His suffering, but He proves it by His continual condescension toward His suffering people in love. You will always find your greatest power to lie in love. There is more eloquence in love than in all the words that the most clever speechmaker can ever put together. We win men's hearts not so much through poetry and by artistic wording of sentences as by the pouring out of a heart's love that makes them feel that we would save them, that we would bless them, that we would, because we belong to them, regard them as brethren and play a brother's part and lay ourselves out to benefit them. Jesus abounds in tenderness, and though He has every other quality to make up a perfect high priest, though He is complete and lacking in nothing, yet if I must mention one thing in which He far outshines us all but in which we should all try to imitate Him, it would be in His tender sympathy to those who are in need.

From the text, I see two things very clearly. *Jesus suffering*: "he himself hath suffered being tempted." *Jesus helping*: "he is able to succor them that are tempted." And then I think I see a third thing most certainly there, namely, *Jesus sought after*: because in the word that is translated *succor*, there is a latent meaning of crying. He is able to hear the cry of those who are tempted. It is a word that signifies a mother's quickness to answer her child's cry, and Jesus is able to answer our cry; therefore we should lift up our cry when our soul is in distress.

Jesus Suffering

I call your attention first to *the feeling* that is expressed: "in that he himself hath suffered being tempted." Many people are tempted yet do not suffer in being tempted. When ungodly men are tempted, the bait is to their liking, and they swallow it greedily. Temptation is a pleasure to them, and they are drawn aside of their own lusts and enticed. Temptation, instead of being suffering to them, becomes a horrible source of pleasure. But good men suffer when they are tempted, and the better they are, the more they suffer. I know some children of God to whom temptation is their constant misery night and day. If it took the form of external affliction, they would bravely bear it; but it takes the shape of evil suggestions and profane insinuations that leap into their minds without their will, although they hate them with their whole heart. These thoughts beset them as a man may be surrounded by swarms of flies from which he cannot get away. Such brethren are tempted, and they suffer being tempted. Our Lord Jesus Christ enters into this trying experience very fully, because His suffering through being tempted must have been much greater than any suffering that the purest-hearted believer can know, seeing that He is more pure than any one of us.

It was a trying thing to the blessed Christ even to dwell here among men. He behaved Himself with most condescending familiarity, but He must have been greatly sickened and saddened by what He saw in this world. Sinners were no fit company for Him, for their views of things and His were as different as possible, and they had no points of agreement in character with Him. They were as much company for Him as a madman to his keeper: they could not come much closer until His grace changed and renewed them. Our Lord and Master had such a delicate sensitiveness of soul with regard to holiness that the sight of sin must have torn Him. There was no callousness about His nature. He had not made Himself familiar with sin by the practice of it, neither had He so associated with those who indulge in evil as to become Himself lenient toward it. We inherit the customs of our ancestors and do not raise questions about that which has been commonly done: we begin at an evil point and start from a wrong point in morals. But not so with our Lord; He had no sin, neither did He learn evil in His upbringing. We also commit sin through a comparative ignorance of its evil, but He knew the horror of it and felt within His soul the shame, the wrong, the inherent baseness of sin against a holy law and a loving God. His infinite knowledge helped Him to understand and measure the heinousness and hell-desert of it, and to be in contact with it must therefore have been a perpetual sorrow to Him. He suffered in being placed where He could be tempted.

When sin actually assailed Him and He was told to prove His Sonship by working to feed Himself, thus anticipating His Father's providence by a hasty act of self-seeking, how He must have loathed the suggestion! When Satan told Him to presumptuously cast Himself down from the temple's pinnacle, how He must have smarted at the horrible proposal! When the tempter hissed in His ear that abominable offer, "All these things will I give thee, if thou wilt fall down and worship me" (Matt. 4:9), it must have grieved the holy heart of Jesus most intensely. He could not yield to temptation, but He did suffer from it. He did not suffer from it morally, for He was too pure for that, but He did suffer from it mentally because of His purity. His mind was grieved and troubled by the temptation that He had to bear. We especially see this when we find Him in the garden of Gethsemane. There He showed His grief when He sweat as it were great drops of blood falling to the ground. In many other ways, He endured such contradiction of sinners against Himself, such multiplied temptations, that it is said by the Holy Spirit in this verse, that He "suffered" being tempted.

Come, then, you who can hardly lift up your heads because of shame as you tremble at the memory of your own thoughts. Come and meet with One who suffered being tempted! He knows how you are hunted by hell dogs, go where you may. He knows that you cannot escape the presence of the tempter, and from His own experience, He enters into your feelings to the full. He gives you a flood of sympathy in these deep distresses of your spirit as you fight against Apollyon and agonize against temptation, for He suffered being tempted.

Let us also consider *the fact* that our Lord was tempted, tempted up to the suffering point. It is not only that *He* suffered being tempted but also that He *Himself* suffered being tempted, showing that the matters were really, truly, personally, actually His. He *Himself* has suffered. All that there was in Him that made up Himself suffered being tempted. Our Lord was tempted by His circumstances, just as you are. He felt the woes of poverty, and poverty at times carried to the extreme. "Foxes have holes, and birds of the air have nests; but the Son of man hath not where to lay his head" (Luke 9:58). He was also weary with incessant labors: "being wearied with his journey, [he] sat thus on the well" (John 4:6). Weariness has its temptations. He who is weary is hardly in the condition to judge things correctly. When we are weary, we are apt to be impatient, complaining, hasty. If you are weary and can hardly keep your eyelids from dropping down, remember before you quite yield to fatigue that your Lord was weary, too. Think of how weary Christ was that He lay down in absolute exhaustion in the ship and could sleep through the worst of storms. Do not blame yourself for feeling tired when you pray or listen to a sermon. I remember how our Lord spoke gently to the disciples when they fell asleep in the garden during His agony. He said, "The spirit indeed is willing, but the flesh is weak" (Matt. 26:41). Jesus would never have thought of so tender an excuse for their untender slumbers if His own flesh had not also been weak when He, too, was weary. The Lord knows from His own circumstances what are the temptations of poverty and weariness. He Himself has hungered, and He said, "I thirst." Everything about Him contributed to fulfill the tale of His trials. He was, above us all, "a man of sorrows, and acquainted with grief" (Isa. 53:3).

And then He suffered from temptations arising from men. He endured sadly much from good men. It would seem that even His beloved mother tried Him. His mother was with His brethren when we read that they were outside, desiring to speak with Him. Was it not at that time that they desired to take Him, for they said, "He is beside himself" (Mark 3:21)? The men of His own family thought that surely He was a man distraught who should be put under restraint. "Neither did his brethren believe in him" (John 7:5).

His disciples, though He loved them so intensely, yet each one tried Him. Even John, the dearest of them all, asked for places at the right and the left hand of His throne for himself and his brother James. Even Peter "took him, and began to rebuke him" (Mark 8:32). All the disciples were of the same mind as Peter when Jesus began to describe His coming crucifixion. Their spirits were often so worldly, so selfish, so foolish, as greatly to grieve their Lord and Leader. While He was the Servant of all, they were seeking who should have the preeminence. When He was seeking the lost, they were calling fire from heaven upon rebels. They spoke unadvisedly with their lips and committed their Lord by their words. And you know how, worst of all, He had to complain in utmost bitterness of spirit: "He that eateth bread with me hath lifted up his heel against me" (John 13:18), so that from the circle of His own favored friends He gathered more thorns than roses. He received wounds in the house of His friends, even as you may have done. Herein you see His power to exhibit sympathy with us. He suffered just as we do by the failures of those whom we love.

As for His enemies, need I speak about them? Did they not all tempt Him? Herodians and Sadducees—the openly skeptical— Pharisees and scribes—the professedly religious—were equally His fierce foes. Those to whom He was a benefactor took up stones again to stone Him, and Jerusalem, over which He had wept, cried,

"Crucify him, crucify him," and would not rest till He was slain. Ah, Lord! We have none of us such foes as You had. However cruel our adversaries, they are not so numerous or so fierce as Yours. Besides, they have some cause to hate *us*, but of Your enemies it is true that they hate You without a cause. They could bring no true charge against Him, and they therefore forged the cruelest of falsehoods until their reproaches broke His heart. So you see how He was tempted and how He suffered.

Moreover, it is a wonderful fact that *He* was tempted of the devil. He in whom all evil is personified dared to stand foot to foot in single duel with Him in whom all goodness is concentrated. The fiend infernal dared to face the God incarnate. God in our mortal flesh encountered the devil in the wilderness of temptation. How could the fiend have ventured to assail our Lord? Truly Lucifer was lifted up to the extreme of pride when he dared to confront his Lord. But Christ was tempted of the devil early in His public career, and again near its close, He exclaimed, "But this is your hour, and the power of darkness" (Luke 22:53). He seemed to hear the dragon's wings as they beat the midnight air, and He cried, "The prince of this world cometh" (John 14:30). Calmly He added, "and hath nothing in me"; yet His heart grew chill in the hideous presence of the great adversary. It was nothing less than an agony in Gethsemane—a painful wrestling between Jesus and the powers of darkness. You who are tempted of the devil; you who are troubled by mysterious whisperings in your ear; you who, when you sing or pray, have a blasphemy suggested to you; you who even in your dreams awake with horror at the thoughts that cross your mind, be comforted, for your Lord knows all your temptation. To you, I say, you can enter into fellowship with your Lord in His being tempted of the devil; that which is incomprehensible to others is plain enough to you.

Beyond that, our Lord knew those temptations that arise out of being deserted by God. There come times to some of us when our soul is cast down within us, when faith becomes feeble and joy languishes, because the light of the divine countenance is withdrawn. We cannot find our God. We enter into the language of Job: "Oh that I knew where I might find him! That I might come even to his seat!" (Job 23:3). We cry with David, "My soul thirsteth for God, for the living God: when shall I come and appear before God? My tears have been my meat day and night, while they continually say unto me, Where is thy God?" (Ps. 42:2–3). Nothing chills the marrow like an eclipse of the great Sun, whose presence makes our day. If the Lord withdraws from us, the strongest faint. In this great temptation, our Lord has suffered His full share. He cried, "Eloi, Eloi, lama sabachthani" (Mark 15:34). There was condensed into that dying cry an infinity of anguish such as we cannot imagine. Some of us know what the surface of this Black Sea is like, but we have never descended into its utmost depths as He did; and if we have done so, this is our comfort—Jesus has been there. He has been to the very bottom of it. He has suffered being tempted even by that heaviest of all trials that ever fall upon the sons of God. There is the fact.

I desire to go a step farther, to comfort you upon *the fruit* of all this, for though our Lord thus suffered being tempted, He suffered not in vain. He was made perfect through His sufferings and was fitted for His solemn office of High Priest to His people. From that fact I want you to gather fruit because our heavenly Father means to bless you also. We cannot comfort others if we have never been comforted ourselves. There is no comforter for a widow like one who has lost her husband. Those who have had no children or have never lost a child may talk very kindly, but they cannot enter into a mother's broken heart who has. If you have never known what temptations mean, you cannot go far in attempting to comfort the tempted. Our Lord obtained a blessing from suffering temptation, and you may do the same. The Lord means to make of you a man that shall be used like Barnabas to be a "son of consolation." He means to make you a mother in Israel who can meet with others who are cast down, and you may know how to drop in a sweet word by which they shall be comforted. Therefore be content to suffer being tempted and look for the comfortable fruit that all this shall produce in you.

Draw from the suffering and temptation of the Lord Jesus the following inferences:

First, that *temptation to sin is no sin*. The fact that Jesus was tempted means that there was no sin in it. You may be horribly tempted, and yet no blame whatever may attach to you, for it is no fault of yours that you are tempted. You need not repent of that which has no sin in it. The mere fact that you are tempted, however horrible the temptation, is no sin of yours unless you yield to it.

Temptation does not show any displeasure on God's part. He permitted His only begotten Son to be tempted: Jesus was always the

Son of His love, and yet He was tried. "This is my beloved Son" (Matt. 3:17), said He at Jesus' baptism, yet the next hour that Son was led of the Spirit into the wilderness to be tempted of the devil. Rather than showing displeasure on God's part, temptation may be consistent with the clearest manifestations of divine favor.

Temptation really implies no doubt of your being a son of God: for *the* Son of God was tempted, even the unquestioned Son of the Highest. The prime model and paragon of sonship, Christ Himself, was tempted. Then why not you? Temptation is a mark of sonship rather than any reflection thereupon.

Temptation need not lead to any evil consequences in any case. It did not in our Lord's case lead to sin. The Lord Jesus was as innocent in temptation and after temptation as before it, and so may we be through His grace. It is written by the beloved John concerning the man who is born of God, that "[he] keepeth himself, and that wicked one toucheth him not" (1 John 5:18).

Moreover, *do not make it any cause of complaint that you are tempted.* If your Lord was tempted, shall the disciple be above his Master? If the Perfect One must endure temptation, why not you? Accept it, therefore, at the Lord's hands and do not think it to be a disgrace or dishonor. The Lord, who sends it, sends also the way of escape, and it will be to your honor and profit to escape by that way.

Never allow temptation to lead you to despair. Jesus did not despair. Jesus triumphed, and so shall you. Therefore He cries, "In the world ye shall have tribulation: but be of good cheer; I have overcome the world" (John 16:33). You are a member of His body, and when the Head wins the victory, the whole body shares the triumph. "Because I live," said He, "ye shall live also" (John 14:19); and so you shall: even in the poisonous atmosphere of temptation you shall be in health. Those of old overcame through the blood of the Lamb, and you shall do the same. Wherefore comfort one another with these words: "He himself hath suffered being tempted." You who have His life in you shall first suffer with Him and then reign with Him.

Jesus Comforting

Jesus suffering is preparatory to Jesus comforting. Observe, then: "He is able to succour them that are tempted." In this we note *His pity,* that He should give Himself up to this business of comforting those who are tempted. Have you a tempted friend living in your house? If so, you have a daily cross to carry, for when we try to comfort others we often become cast down ourselves, and the temptation is for us to get rid of them or keep out of their way. Has it never occurred to you this way? But our Lord is so caring that He seeks out those who are cast down, and He heals the brokenhearted and binds up their wounds. He reaches out to those who are tempted and never hides from them or passes them by on the other side. What an example is this for us! He devotes Himself to this divine business of comforting all such as mourn. He is Lord of all, yet He makes Himself the servant of the weakest. Whatever He may do with the strongest, He comforts "them that are tempted." He does not throw up His hands in disgust or grow angry with them because they are so foolish as to give way to idle fears. He does not tell them that it is all their nerves and that they are stupid and silly and should shake themselves out of such nonsense. I have often heard people talk like this, and I have half wished that they had felt a little twinge of depression themselves, just to put them into a more tender state of heart. The Lord Jesus never overdrives a lame sheep, but He sets the bone and carries the sheep on His shoulders, so tenderly compassionate is He. Here is His pity.

By His own sufferings, Jesus has *the right* to enter in among sufferers and deal with them in comfort. And He also has the right because He has bought them with His blood. The feeble, the weak, the trembling, the desponding are in His care, committed to Him by God. He said, "Fear not, little flock" (Luke 12:32), which shows that His flock is little and timid. He says these words of comfort because the flock has a great tendency to fear and because He does not like to see them so troubled. He has bought them, and so He has the right to comfort them and preserve them to the end.

He has also *the disposition* to comfort them. He obtained that tender temper through suffering by being Himself tempted. The man who has seen affliction, when he is blessed of God, has the disposition to cheer those who are afflicted. Jesus having been tempted at all points as His children, His trials have become the means to blessing those who are tried.

And then He has the special *ability*. "He is able to succor them that are tempted." There are certain people whom I do not wish to be near when I am sick. They talk so loudly and roughly that my head aches; they say things, though they are meant to be kind, that are the sort of remarks that pour vinegar into my wounds; they have a way of stomping across the floor and banging doors that puts my nerves on end. They do not understand the condition of the sufferer, and so they say all their words the wrong way. If Christians are to be comforters, they must learn the art of comforting by being themselves tried. They cannot learn it any other way. Our Blessed Master, having lived a life of suffering, understands the condition of a sufferer so well that He knows how to deal with us in the weakness and pain of our affliction. He has become so divine a Physician, so tender a Sympathizer, because He has passed through our sorrow. "In all their affliction he was afflicted" (Isa. 63:9).

Our Lord has many ways of comforting those who are tempted. Usually He comforts the tempted by giving them a sense of His sympathy. They say, "Yes, my Lord is here. He feels for me." That is in itself a comfort of no small order. Sometimes He comforts them by suggesting to them precious truths that are the sweet antidote for the poison of sorrow. There is in the Bible a remedy exactly fitted for your grief if you could only find it. The Bible contains keys that will open the iron gates of your trouble and give you freedom from your sorrow. The point is to find out the right promises. And the Spirit of God often helps us in that matter by bringing the words of the Lord Jesus to our remembrance. We would have never known the richness of the Word of God had it not been that in our varied distress the Lord has shown us how He foresaw all and provided for all in the covenant of promise.

The Lord also comforts His people by inwardly strengthening them. How often have we heard people say, "I never dreamed I could bear up to the trial." Yes, through grace, a secret divine energy is poured into the soul. We are treated, as John Bunyan put it, by secret supplies of grace imparted in a hidden manner. We are like a fire that has water poured on it and yet keeps burning. Behind the wall another person is secretly pouring oil on the fire, so it still keeps burning.

I have known the Lord to bless His people by making them very weak. The next best thing to being strong in the Lord is to be extremely weak in yourself. They go together, but sometimes they are divided in experience. It is grand to feel, "I will not struggle with this anymore. I will give it all up and lie quietly in the Lord's hands." It is the sweetest feeling, I think, outside of heaven! As in the center of a hurricane there is a spot where there is perfect calm, so there is, in a deep sense of yielding up to God, in the very center of your pain and your grief and your misery and your depression a place of perfect repose when you have once yielded yourself fully up to God.

Jesus Sought After

Let us seek Him. Come, you who are weary, come to Him who is able to comfort you. Do not stay away until you are a little comforted, but come in your despair. Do not wait until you have a little more faith, but come just as you are and say to Him, "Dear Lord, You have felt all this, and I lie down at Your dear feet! Do help me!" Let these few thoughts help to bring you now in prayer and trust and hope to the feet of this Great High Priest.

Where else can you go? Who can help a soul like you? Come to Him, then. Men are like cisterns that are all broken. Come to the fountain. Come to my Lord. Every other door is shut, but yet you may not despair, for He says, "Behold, I have set before thee an open door" (Rev. 3:8).

Where better can you go? Do you want to find a friend able to help you? To whom should you go but to your own Lord, the sympathizing Son of Man? To whom better can you go? Do you say that you are downcast? Do you tell me you are afraid you are not a child of God? Never mind about that. Come as a sinner if you cannot come as a saint. Do you mourn that you have evil thoughts? Come and confess your bad ones. Do you lament that you are not brokenhearted for sin, as you should be? Come, then, to be brokenhearted. Do you mourn that you are unspeakably bad? Then come at your worst. If you want a surgeon, it is never a good thing to say, "My bone is broken, but I shall not have it set until it begins to mend." Go while it is broken! Cry to the Savior! Ask Him to save you now. Remember that He never cast anyone out. Never yet! Never one!

Come, then, just as you are, saint or sinner, whoever you may be. Have done with yourself, your good self and your bad self, too, and say, "If I perish, I will trust in Jesus." Trust in Jesus, and you cannot perish. If you perish believing in Jesus, I must perish with you. You may be a very seasick passenger, and I may be an able-bodied seaman, but if you are drowned, I shall be, for I cannot swim anymore than you can. I depend upon the seaworthiness of this vessel of free grace in which we are embarked, and we must either reach heaven together or we sink together. And when we get there, you and I, poor broken-down one, oh, will we not sing? Will we not sing aloud and clash the high-sounding cymbals with all our might? I will contend with you as to which shall praise God most. You say that you will. I say that I shall. Will we not vie with each other and with all the redeemed ones to sing Hallelujah to God and the Lamb? If ever such sinners as you and I get inside the gates of heaven, we will give forth such outcries of holy joy and gladness as never came from angels' throats but can come only from the lips of sinners bought with blood.

The Lord, who comforts the tempted, Himself bless and comfort you!

*M*ingled with this anger was grief. Jesus was heartbroken because their hearts were so hard. As Manton puts it, "He was softened because of their hardness." His was not the pitiless flame of wrath that burns in a dry eye; He had tears as well as anger. His thunderstorm brought a shower of pity with it. The Greek word is hard to translate. There was a togetherness in the word; He grieved with them. He felt that the hardness of their hearts would one day bring upon them an awful misery, and foreseeing that coming grief, He grieved with them by way of anticipation. He was grieved at their hardness because it would injure them; their blind enmity vexed Him because it was securing their own destruction. He was angry because they were willfully rejecting the light that would have illuminated them with heavenly brightness, the life that could have quickened them into fullness of joy. They were determinedly and resolutely destroying their own souls out of hatred for Him, and He was angry more for their sakes than for His own.

Chapter Eleven

Jesus Angry With Hard Hearts

And when he had looked round about on them with anger, being grieved for the hardness of their hearts, he saith unto the man, Stretch forth thine hand. And he stretched it out: and his hand was restored whole as the other—Mark 3:5.

IT IS THE DIVINE LORD, the compassionate Jesus, the meek and lowly in heart, who is here described as being angry. Where else do we meet with such a statement while He was here among men? A poor man was present in the synagogue who had a withered hand. It was his right hand, and he who has to earn his daily bread can guess what it must be to have that hand paralyzed or damaged. In the same synagogue was the Savior, ready to restore to that hand all its strength and dexterity. The company that had gathered in the synagogue, professedly to worship God, would they not have special cause to do so when they saw a miracle of divine goodness? I can imagine them whispering one to another, "We shall see our poor neighbor restored today, for the Son of God has come among us with power to heal, and He will make this a very glorious Sabbath by His work of gracious power."

But I must not let imagination mislead me. They did nothing of the kind. Instead, they sat watching the Lord Jesus, not to be delighted by an act of His power but to find something by which they might accuse Him. When all was said and done, the utmost that they would be able to allege would be that He had healed a withered hand *on the Sabbath*. Overlooking the commendation due for the miracle of healing, they laid the emphasis upon its being done on the Sabbath and held up their hands with horror that such a secular action should be performed on such a sacred day. Now, the Savior puts very plainly before them the question, "Is it lawful to do good on the sabbath days?" (vs. 4). He put it in a form that allowed only one reply. The question could, no doubt, have been easily answered by these scribes and Pharisees, but then their answer would have condemned them, and therefore they were all as mute as mice. Scribes most skilled in splitting hairs and Pharisees who could measure the border of a garment to the eighth of an inch declined to answer one of the simplest questions in morals. Mark describes the Savior as looking around upon them all with anger and grief, as well He might.

Mark is descriptive to the last degree in his record of this incident. By the help of Mark's clear words you can easily picture the Savior looking round upon them. Jesus stands up boldly, as one who has nothing to hide, as one who is about to do that which would need no defense. He challenged observation, though He knew that His opposition to ecclesiastical authority would involve His own death and hasten the hour of the cross. He did not defy them, but He did make them feel their insignificance as He stood looking round. Can you imagine the power of that look? The look of a man who is much given to anger has little force in it: it is the blaze of a wisp of straw, fierce and short. In many cases we almost smile at the impotent rage that looks out from angry eyes; but a gentle spirit, like the Savior's, commands reverence if once moved to indignation. His meek and lowly heart could have been stirred with anger only by some overwhelming cause.

Even when moved to an indignant look, His anger ended there. He only looked, but spoke no word of upbraiding. And the look itself had in it more of pity than of contempt, more of compassion than of passion. Our Lord's look upon the assembly of opponents deserves our sincere regard. Jesus paused long enough in that survey to gaze upon each person and to let him know what was intended by the glance. Nobody escaped the searching light that that expressive eye flashed upon each malicious watcher. Each saw that to Him his conduct was loathsome. Jesus understood them and was deeply moved by their obstinacy.

Note well that Jesus did not speak a word, and yet He said more without words than another man could have said with them. The people were not worthy of a word; neither would more words have had the slightest effect upon them. Jesus saved His words for the poor man with the withered hand, but for these people, a look was the best reply. They looked on Him, and now He looked on them. Concentrated love dwells in the face of Jesus, the Judge, and something of the wrath of the Lion of the Tribe of Judah was seen in Jesus' face. I wish I had skill to describe our Lord's look, but I leave that to your imagination.

When Mark has told us of that look, he proceeds to mention the mingled feelings that were revealed by it. In that look were two things—anger and grief, indignation and inward sorrow. "He looked round about on them with anger, being grieved for the hardness of their hearts." He was angry that they should willingly blind their eyes to a truth so plain, an argument so convincing. He had put to them a question to which there could be only one answer, and they would not give it. He had thrown light in their eyes, and they would not see it. He had utterly destroyed their chosen pretext for opposition, and yet they would persist in opposing Him. Evidently it is possible to be angry and to be right. Hard to many is the precept, "Be angry, and sin not" (Eph. 4:26). And this fact renders the Savior's character all the more admirable, since He so easily accomplished what is so difficult to us. He could be angry with sin and yet never cease to be compassionate to the sinner. His was not anger that desired evil to its object; it was simply love on fire, love burning with indignation against that which is unlovely.

Mingled with this anger was grief. Jesus was heartbroken because their hearts were so hard. As Manton puts it, "He was softened because of their hardness." His was not the pitiless flame of wrath that burns in a dry eye; He had tears as well as anger. His thunderstorm brought a shower of pity with it. The Greek word is hard to translate. There was *a togetherness* in the word; He grieved with them. He felt that the hardness of their hearts would one day bring upon them an awful misery, and foreseeing that coming grief, He grieved with them by way of anticipation. He was grieved at their hardness because it would injure them; their blind enmity vexed Him because it was securing their own destruction. He was angry because they were willfully rejecting the light that would have illuminated them with heavenly brightness, the life that could have quickened them into fullness of joy. They were determinedly and resolutely destroying their own souls out of hatred for Him, and He was angry more for their sakes than for His own.

If I had been one of the disciples who were with Him in the synagogue, I think I would have burned with indignation to see them refusing to forgo their hate of Jesus and yet be unable to say a word in defense of it. What a horrible thing that any creature in the shape of a man should act so unworthily to the blessed Son of God as to blame Him for doing good! What a disgrace to our race for men to be so inhuman as to wish to see their fellow man's hand remain withered and to dare to blame the gentle Physician who was about to make him perfectly whole! Man is indeed at enmity with God when he finds an argument for hate in a deed of love.

What Caused This Anger and Grief

It was their hardness of heart, the callousness of their conscience, their utter lack of feeling. Their hearts had lost their proper softness. As a person who takes deadly drugs little by little until his system has been hardened against the drugs' result, hardening of the heart is the worst kind. The heart should be all tenderness, and when it is not, the life must be coarse and evil. Yet multitudes are morally smitten with ossification of the heart. A heart of flesh may be gone out of a man, and instead he may have a heart of stone. Scripture even calls it "an adamant stone"—unfeeling, unyielding, impenetrable, obstinate. Those enemies of our Lord who sat in the synagogue that Sabbath day were incorrigible; they strengthened their hatred of Him in the resolve that they would not be convinced no matter what He said or did. Our Lord Jesus became angry, grieved, and sorrowful with them.

What was their exact fault?

First, *they would not see*, though the case was clear. Jesus had set the truth so plainly before them that they were obliged to strain their understandings to avoid being convinced. They had to draw down the blinds of the soul and put up the shutters of the mind to be able *not* to see. There are none so blind as those who will not see, and these were of that blindest order. They were blind people who had eyes and boasted that they could see, and therefore their sin was utterly without excuse.

What was more, *what these people were forced to see they would not acknowledge*. They sullenly held their tongues when they were bound to speak. Does it not happen to many people that the gospel forces itself upon their belief? They feel that they could not conjure up an argument against the divine truth that is set before them. The word comes with such demonstration that it strikes them with sledgehammer force. But they do not intend to admit its power, and so they brace themselves up to bear the blow without yielding. They shut their mouths against the water of life that is held up to them in the golden cup of the gospel. There sat these scribes and Pharisees. It is a wonder that the stones did not cry out against them, they were so doggedly determined not to admit that which they could not deny.

More than that, *while they would not see what was so plain, they were diligently seeking to spy out flaws and faults where there were none, namely, in the Lord Jesus.* So there are many who profess that they cannot understand the gospel, but they have understanding enough to cavil at it and cast slurs upon it. They have a cruelly keen eye for nonexistent errors in Scripture: they find this mistake in Deuteronomy and another in Genesis. What great wisdom, to be diligent in making discoveries against one's own eternal interests! The gospel of the Lord Jesus is man's only hope of salvation: what a pity to count it the height of cleverness to destroy our only hope! Alas, for the captious skeptics! They are sharp-sighted as eagles against themselves, but they are blind as bats to those things that make for their peace. These religious leaders tried to find fault in Jesus, and yet they could not or would not see the wickedness of their own opposition to Him.

They dared to sit in judgment upon the Lord, who proved Himself by His miracles to be divine, and yet all the while they professed great reverence for God and His law. Though they were fighting against God, they made the pretense of being very zealous for Him, and especially for His holy day. This is an old trick of Satan, to fight true religion with false religion, to battle godliness in the name of orthodoxy. This is a hollow sham, and we do not wonder that our ever truthful Lord felt indignant at it.

Our Lord Jesus cannot endure hypocrites. He cares not for whitewashed sepulchers but proclaims woe to all false professors. Those who are dead while they live, having a form of godliness but denying the power of it, present a fair outside but secretly practice all manner of abominations. What have they to do in the Church of

God? What a horror to know that there are such in the assemblies of the saints! Dread the hardness that would permit you to be a hypocrite. Shun above all things that deadness of soul that makes a false profession possible, for this is very grievous to the Lord.

A hard heart is insensible, impenetrable, inflexible. You can no more affect it than if you should strike your hand against a stone wall. Satan has fortified it and made its possessor to be steadfast, unmoveable, always abounding in the works of sin. The enmity of such a heart leads it to resist all that is good. Its hardness returns the efforts of love in the form of opposition. Our Savior saw before Him persons who would oppose Him whatever He did and would not change their minds however they might be made to see their error.

Is There Anything of This in Our Hearts?

It is possible to have a hard heart and be very respectable people. We may go to the synagogue, as they did; we may be Bible readers, as the scribes were; we may practice all the outward forms of religion, as the Pharisees did; and yet the Lord Jesus may be grieved with us because of the hardness of our heart.

We may anger the Lord and yet be strictly noncommittal. Jesus was angry that men should be silent when honesty and candor demanded speech of them. You must not think you can escape by saying, "I am not a professing believer." There can be no third party in this case. In the eternal world there is no provision made for neutrals. Those who are not with Jesus are against Him, and they that gather not with Him are scattering abroad. You are either wheat or tares, and there is nothing between the two.

You may be very tender toward other people, and yet you may be so fond of pleasing others that you cannot please the Lord. Such people have not the moral courage to oppose anyone for the sake of truth. This may well cause Jesus to look upon you with anger and grief, as your fear of speaking the truth is driving you to spiritual suicide. To save you a little present discomfort, you are heaping up wrath and judgment.

This hardness of heart may be in us, though we may have occasional meltings! I think that man has a very hard heart who is at times deeply moved but violently represses his emotions. He hurries home to an inner room greatly distressed, but in a short time he shakes off his fears. He goes to a funeral and trembles on the brink of the grave but joins his merry companions and is soon at his sins again. He likes to hear a stirring sermon, but he is careful to not go beyond his depth while hearing it. By a desperate resolve he holds out against the pressure of the grace of God as it comes to him in exhortations and entreaties. It shows an awful vitality of evil when you have been driven to the verge of repentance and then have deliberately turned back to the way of evil, sinning against conscience and conviction.

It is possible to have a hard heart and yet keep clear of gross sins. It is quite possible to guard yourself in certain directions and yet be lax in other matters. Some have gone to excess in sins against God yet have been scrupulous in avoiding sins toward man. Your outwardly moral man is often a hardened rebel against God. His pride of character helps to harden him against the gospel of peace. He condemns others who are really no worse than himself. There is an abominable kind of prudence that keeps some men out of certain sins: they are too mean to be prodigal, too fond of ease to plunge into risky sins. Many a man is carried off his feet by a sudden flood of temptation and sins grievously, and yet at heart he may be by no means so hardened as the cool, calculating transgressor. Woe to the man who has learned to sin deliberately and to measure out iniquity as if it were a lawful merchandise to be weighed by the ounce and the pound! For them there will be reserved the deeper hell, though they escape present condemnation.

Hardness of heart creeps over men by insensible degrees. The hardest hearted man in the world was not so once; the flesh of his heart was petrified little by little. He who can now curse and blaspheme once wept for his boyish faults at his mother's knee and would have shuddered at the simple thought of falling asleep without a prayer. There are those who would give worlds to be free from the bondage of habit so as to feel as once they did. Their soul is as parched as the Sahara; it has forgotten the dew of tears. Their heart is hot as an oven with evil passions, and no soft breath of holy penitence ever visits it. Oh, that they could weep! Oh, that they could feel! Repentance is hid from their eyes. There remains nothing sensitive about them, except it is the base imitation of it that comes over them when they are in a drunken state. What calamity can be greater? What can be said of sin that is more terrible than that it hardens and deadens? Well did the apostle say, "Exhort one another daily, while it is called To day; lest any of you be hardened through the deceitfulness of sin" (Heb. 3:13).

Among the hardened are some who may be said especially to provoke the Lord. Some have received an unusually keen moral sense but have blunted it by repeated sin. Esau was all the more a "profane person" because he was the son of Isaac, knowing something about the covenant heritage, and had certain fine touches of nature that should have made him a better man. This is also true of those who have been indulged by providence with good health, prosperous businesses, and a fine family around them. They have all they can wish for, and yet God receives from them no gratitude. Indeed, they hardly give him a thought. Ingratitude is sure to bring a curse upon the man guilty of it. If there is an honest heart in you, your heart would cleave to the Lord in deep and hearty love. Silken cords of love are stronger with true men than fetters of iron are to thieves.

Other persons have endured many trials, often suffered pain of body, and been brought at times to the verge of the grave; yet, after all, they are hard of heart. The fire of affliction has not softened their iron nature. The Lord Himself cries, "O Ephraim, what shall I do unto thee?" (Hos. 6:4). Long-suffering fails; mercy is weary. There are no more rods to use upon you; as the bullock kicks against the goad, so do you resist the chastening of the Lord God. The Savior looks upon all such with that grieving anger of which the text speaks.

Some have been the subjects of tender, sincere, faithful ministry. Whether from a loving mother or a wise father, a caring teacher or the witness of a minister, very select have been the agencies used upon you. Choice and musical the voices that have endeavored to charm you. If they do not reach you, neither would you be converted though one rose from the dead. If Jesus Himself were here again among men, how could even He reach you? If all the means He has already used have failed with you, I know not what is to be done with you. The Savior Himself will, I fear, leave you; with a look of grief and anger He will turn from you because of the hardness of your heart. Stay, Lord Jesus, stay a little longer! Perhaps they will be won next time. Bid not Your Spirit take His everlasting flight.

What Should Be Our Feeling in Reference to This?

First, *let us renounce forever the habit of criticism.* These scribes and Pharisees were great word spinners, critics, faultfinders. They found fault with the Savior for healing on the Sabbath; He had not broken God's law of the Sabbath, He had only exposed their error upon that point. If the Sabbath had not furnished an opportunity for objection, they would soon have found another, for they meant to object. Multitudes of people in this present day are most effectually hardening their hearts by this same habit. While others are struck by the beauty of the gospel that they hear, these people remember only a mispronunciation made by the preacher. They begin to sit in judgment on the gospel preached, and before long, the Scriptures themselves are subjected to their alteration and correction. Reverence is gone, and self-sufficiency reigns. They criticize God's Word. Any fool can do that, but only a fool will do it. They give themselves the airs of literary men; they are not like ordinary hearers; they require something more intellectual. They look down with contempt upon people who enjoy the gospel and are proving the power of it in their lives. They themselves are persons of remarkable mind, men of light and leading, and it gives them distinction to act the part of skeptics. They show their great learning by turning up their noses at the plain teaching of the Bible. It seems to be a great feature of a cultured man to wear a sneer upon his face when he meets with believers in inspiration. Pride of this sort ruins those who indulge it. To be unbelieving in order to show one's superiority is an unsatisfactory business.

Let us never imitate that evil spirit who in the garden of Eden proved himself to be the patron and exemplar of all skeptics. Remember how he raised the question, "Yea, hath God said?"(Gen. 3:1). Forget not how he went further and, like a sage philosopher, hinted that there was a larger hope: "Ye shall not surely die," said he (vs. 4). Then he advanced to lay down a daring, radical philosophy and whispered, "God doth know that in the day ye eat thereof, then your eyes shall be opened, and ye shall be as gods"(vs. 5). This old serpent has left his trail on many minds at the present time, and you can see it in the slimy questions and poisonous suggestions of the age. Get away from criticism: it is of all labors the least remunerative.

Next, *let us feel an intense desire to submit ourselves to the Lord Jesus.* If He is in the synagogue, let us ask Him to heal us and to do it in His own way. Let us become His disciples and follow Him wherever He leads. Yield yourself to God. Be as melted wax to the seal. Be as the water of the lake that is moved with every breath of the wind. All He wills is our salvation. Lord Jesus, let Your will be done!

Let us be careful to keep away from all hardening influences, whether of books or men or habits or pleasures. If there is any influence that deadens us to spiritual things, that hinders our prayers, shakes our faith, or dampens our zeal, let us get out of it and keep out of it. If any pleasure lessens our hatred of sin, let us never go near it; if any book clouds our view of Jesus, let us never read it. We grow hard soon enough through the necessary contact with the world that arises through our normal life; let us not increase these evils. Shun the idler's talk, the scorner's seat, and the way of the ungodly. Be sincere and pure; live near to God and move far away from the throne of iniquity.

Last, *use all softening influences.* Ask to have your heart daily rendered sensitive by the indwelling of the Holy Spirit. Go often to read and hear the Word: it is like a fire and like a hammer breaking the rock in pieces. Dwell at the foot of the cross; it is there that tenderness is born into human hearts. Jesus makes all hearts soft, and then He stamps His image on them. Entreat the Holy Spirit to give you a very vivid sense of sin and a very intense dread of it. If such is the condition of our heart, our Lord will not be angry with us. He will look around upon us with joy and take delight in us.

He who made the heart can melt it. Job said, "God maketh my heart soft" (Job 23:16). It is the special office of the Holy Spirit to renew our nature. The Holy Spirit can work in us conviction of sin, the new birth, faith in the Lord Jesus, deep contrition, and holy tenderness. "A new heart also will I give you, and a new spirit will I put within you: and I will take away the stony heart out of your flesh, and I will give you an heart of flesh" (Ezek. 36:26). That kind of heart that you so greatly need shall be given you, though indeed it is a miracle of miracles to do it. A new arm or leg would be a wonder, but what shall be said of a new heart? The spirit that you also so greatly require is to be bestowed; your whole tone, temper, and tendency shall be altered in an extraordinary manner. Do you think then that it can never be done in your case? Remember that the Lord never speaks beyond His ability. His arm has not grown short so that He cannot save to the uttermost. The Lord can fill up the empty spaces of the heart with the most gentle and sensitive affections. Instead of needing to be smitten with a hammer, we shall feel the slightest touch of the divine finger and shall answer to the faintest call of the divine voice. What a change!

*M*any days have passed since then, and I ask you now to recall what Christ has done to us since we first trusted in Him. Has His love for you cooled in the slightest degree? We have all tried that love by our wandering and waywardness, but we have not quenched it, and its fire still burns just as vehemently as at the first. We have sometimes fallen so low that our hearts have been like stone, incapable of emotion, yet Jesus has loved us all the while and softened our hard hearts as the glorious sun melts the icebergs of the ocean. We were like the insensible grass that calls not for the dew, yet the dew of His love gently fell upon us; though we had not sought it, our heart was refreshed by it. Our Lord has indeed proven how He loves us by the gracious way in which He has borne with our many provocations; and think too, with what gifts He has enriched us, with what comforts He has sustained us, with what divine energy He has renewed our failing strength, and with what blessed guidance He has led and is still leading us! Try to set down in words the total indebtedness of your heart to His love: where will you begin, and when you have begun, where will you finish? If you were to record only one out of a million of His gifts of love, would the whole world be able to contain the books that might be written concerning them? "Behold how he loved us!"

Chapter Twelve

Oh, How He Loves!

Then said the Jews, Behold how he loved him!—John 11:36.

It was at the grave of Lazarus that Jesus wept, and His grief was so manifest to the onlookers that they said, "Behold how he loved him!" Those of us who have a share in the special love of Jesus see evidences of that love not only in His tears but also in the precious blood that He so freely shed for us. We should marvel even more than those Jews did at the love of Jesus and see further into His heart than they did and know more of Him than they could in the brief interval in which they had become acquainted with Him. When we think of His love, we may well cry, "Behold how he loved us!"

These Jews expressed their wonder at the love that Jesus had for His friend Lazarus. In these days, we are too apt to repress our emotions. While I do not greatly admire the enthusiastic noise that is raised in some places during a church service, I would rather have that than to have people holding themselves back from uttering their heart's true feelings. If our heart is right, we should often be saying to one another, "How wondrous has the love of Jesus been to us!" We waste far too much of our time upon trifles; it would be well if the love of Jesus so engrossed our thoughts that it engrossed our conversations as well.

What the Love of Christ Has Done for Us

When did Christ's love begin to work for us? It was long before we were born, long before the world was created; far, far back, *in eternity, our Savior gave the first proof of His love to us by espousing our cause.* By His divine foresight, He looked upon human nature as a palace that had been plundered and broken down, and in its ruins He perceived all kinds of unclean things. Who was there to undertake the great work of restoring that ruined palace? No one but the Word, who was with God, and who was God. "And he saw that there was no man, and wondered that there was no intercessor: therefore his arm brought salvation unto him; and his righteousness, it sustaineth him" (Isa. 59:16). Before the angels began to sing or the sun and moon and stars threw their first beams through primeval darkness, Christ espoused the cause of His people and resolved not only to restore to them all the blessings that He foresaw that they would lose but also to add to them richer favors than could ever have been theirs except through Him. Even from eternity His delights were with the sons of men. And when I think of Him, in that far-distant past of which we can form so slight a conception, becoming "the head over all things to the church" (Eph. 1:22), which then existed only in the mind of God, my very soul cries out in a rapture of delight, "Behold how he loved us!"

Remember, too, that *in that eternal secret council, the Lord Jesus Christ became the Representative and Surety of His chosen people.* There was to be, in what was then the far remote future, a covenant between God and man. But who was there who was both able and willing to sign that covenant on man's behalf and to give a guarantee that man's part of that covenant should be fulfilled? Then it was that the Son of God, knowing all that such a suretyship would involve, undertook to be the Surety for His people, to fulfill the covenant on their behalf, and to meet all its demands that He foresaw that they would be unable to meet. Then the eternal Father gave into Christ's charge the souls that He had chosen for eternal life, and the eternal Son covenanted to redeem all those souls after they had fallen through sin, to keep them by His grace, and to present them "faultless" before the presence of His Father with exceeding joy. Thus, Jesus Christ, "that great shepherd of the sheep, through the blood of the everlasting covenant" (Heb. 13:20), undertook to redeem and guard the whole flock entrusted to His care so that not one of them should be missing and the blessed Shepherd-Son should be able to say to His Father, "Those that thou gavest me I have kept, and none of them is lost" (John 17:12). It was in the everlasting covenant that our Lord Jesus Christ became our Representative and Surety and engaged on our behalf to fulfill all His Father's will. As we think of this great mystery of mercy, surely we should exclaim with grateful adoration, "Behold how he loved us!"

In the fullness of time, *our Lord Jesus Christ left the glories of heaven and took upon Him our nature.* We know so little of what *heaven* means that we cannot adequately appreciate the tremendous sacrifice that the Son of God must have made to become the son of Mary. The holy angels could understand far better than we can what their Lord and ours gave up when He renounced the royalties of heaven, and all the honor and glory that rightly belonged to Him as the Son of the Highest, and left His throne and crown above to be born as the babe of an earthly mother, yet there were mysteries about His incarnation that even they could not fathom. As they followed the footprints of the Son of man on His wondrous way from the manger to the cross and to the tomb, they must often have been in that most suggestive attitude of which Peter wrote, "which things the angels desire to look into" (1 Pet. 1:12). To us, the incarnation of Christ is one of the greatest marvels of the history of the universe, and we say with Paul, "Without controversy great is the mystery of godliness" (1 Tim. 3:16). The omnipotent Creator took the nature of the creature into indissoluble union with His divine nature; and, marvel of marvels, that creature was man. For an angel to become a cat, if that were possible, would be nothing at all in comparison with the condescension of Christ in becoming the babe of Bethlehem, for an angel and a cat are only creatures formed by Christ. O glorious Bridegroom of our hearts, there never was any other love like Yours! That the eternal Son of God should leave His Father's side and stoop so low as to become one of His chosen people, so that Paul could truly write, "We are members of his body, of his flesh, and of his bones" (Eph. 5:30), is such a wonder of condescending grace and mercy that we can only exclaim, "Behold how he loved us!"

Then, "being found in fashion as a man" (Phil 2:8), *He took upon*

Himself human sickness and suffering. All our infirmities that were not sinful Jesus Christ endured—the weary feet, the aching head, and the throbbing heart, "that it might be fulfilled which was spoken by Isaiah the prophet, saying, Himself took our infirmities, and bare our sickness" (Matt. 8:17). This was a wondrous proof of love, that the ever-blessed Son of God, who needed not to suffer, should have been willing to be hampered with infirmity just like any other man is. "For we have not an high priest which cannot be touched with the feeling of our infirmities; but was in all points tempted like as we are, yet without sin" (Heb. 4:15).

But if you want to see the love of Jesus at the highest point it ever reached, you must, by faith, gaze upon Him when *He took upon Himself the sins of all His people,* as Peter writes, "Who his own self bare our sins in his own body on the tree" (1 Pet. 2:24). How could one who was so pure, so absolutely perfect, ever bear so foul a load? Yet He did bear it, and the transfer of His people's sin from them to Him was so complete that the inspired prophet wrote, "The Lord hath laid on him the iniquity of us all" (Isa. 53:6), and the inspired apostle wrote, "For he hath made him to be sin for us, who knew no sin; that we might be made the righteousness of God in him" (2 Cor. 5:21). When Christ took the Church into an eternal marriage union with Himself, although she had incurred such liabilities as could not have been paid if she had spent all eternity in hell, He took all her debts upon Himself and then paid them to the uttermost penny. For we must never forget that when Christ bore His people's sins, He also bore the full punishment of them. In fulfillment of the great eternal covenant and in prospect of all the glory and blessing that would follow from Christ's atoning sacrifice, "it pleased the Lord to bruise him; he hath put him to grief" (Isa. 53:10). We cannot have the slightest idea of what that bruising and grief must have been. We do not fathom His soul agony that made Him cry, "My God, my God, why hast thou forsaken me?" (Matt. 27:46). I cannot write of this wondrous mystery as I would hope, but you who know even in part what it means must join me in saying, "Behold how he loved us!"

Further than that, *Christ has so completely given Himself to us that all that He has is ours.* He is the glorious Husband, and His Church is His bride, the Lamb's wife. There is nothing that He has that is not all hers even now and that He will not share with her forever. By a marriage bond that cannot be broken, He has taken her to

Himself in righteousness and truth, and she shall be one with Him throughout eternity. He has gone up to His Father's house to take possession of the many mansions there, not for Himself but for His people, and His constant prayer is, "Father, I will that they also, whom thou hast given me, be with me where I am; that they may behold my glory, which thou hast given me: for thou lovedst me before the foundation of the world" (John 17:24). Jesus has an ever-flowing fountain of joy in His heart, but He desires that His joy may be in you if you belong to Him and that your joy may be full; and everything else that He has is yours as much as it is His, so surely you will join with me in saying, "Behold how he loved us!"

What Christ Has Done to Us

Think *how the Lord dealt with us before we came to Him*. He called us again and again, but we would not go to Him; and the more lovingly He called us, the more resolutely we hardened our hearts and refused to accept His gracious invitation. This refusal may have lasted for years, and we wonder now that the Lord waited for us so long. Jesus refused to take our no for an answer but called and called again and again, until at last we could hold out no longer and had to yield to the sweet compulsion of His grace. Do you remember how you received pardon, justification, adoption, the indwelling of the Spirit, and how the many "exceeding great and precious promises" (2 Pet. 1:4) were brought to you, like the various courses at a royal festival served upon golden dishes adorned with priceless gems? Oh, that blessed, blessed day in which you first came and sat among the guests at the King's table! Surely your heart glows in grateful remembrance of Christ's mercy, and you cannot help saying, "Behold how he loved us!"

Many days have passed since then, and I ask you now to recall *what Christ has done to us since we first trusted in Him*. Has His love for you cooled in the slightest degree? We have all tried that love by our wandering and waywardness, but we have not quenched it, and its fire still burns just as vehemently as at the first. We have sometimes fallen so low that our hearts have been like stone, incapable of emotion, yet Jesus has loved us all the while and softened our hard hearts as the glorious sun melts the icebergs of the ocean. We were like the insensible grass that calls not for the dew, yet the dew of His love gently fell upon us; though we had not sought it, our heart was refreshed by it. Our Lord has indeed proven how He loves us by the gracious way in which He has borne with our many provocations; and think too, with what gifts He has enriched us, with what comforts He has sustained us, with what divine energy He has renewed our failing strength, and with what blessed guidance He has led and is still leading us! Try to set down in words the total indebtedness of your heart to His love: where will you begin, and when you have begun, where will you finish? If you were to record only one out of a million of His gifts of love, would the whole world be able to contain the books that might be written concerning them? "Behold how he loved us!"

There have been times when we have seemed to stand in the very suburbs of heaven, where we could hear the bells ringing forth celestial music from the invisible belfries, and our hearts were ravished with the sound of the heavenly harpers harping with their harps and the ten thousand times ten thousand white-robed choristers singing the song of Moses and of the Lamb. No, more than that, the King Himself has brought us into His banqueting house, and His banner over us has been love. He not only has permitted us to sit at His feet, as Mary did, but also has allowed us to rest our head on His bosom, as John did, and even condescended to let us put our finger into the print of the nails in our rapturous familiar fellowship with Him who is not ashamed to call us His brethren. Again we must say, "Behold how he loved us!"

One last proof of Christ's love is that *He has made us long for heaven and given us at least a measure of preparation for it.* We are expecting that one of these days, if the chariots and horses of fire do not stop at our door, our dear Lord and Savior will fulfill to us His promise: "If I go and prepare a place for you, I will come again, and receive you unto myself; that where I am, there ye may be also" (John 14:3). To a true believer in Jesus, the thought of departing from this world and going to be with the Lord has nothing of gloom associated with it. This earth is the place of our exile; heaven is our home. We are like the loving wife who is separated by thousands of miles of sea and land from her dear husband, and we are longing for the great reunion with our beloved Lord, from whom we shall then never again be separated. I cannot hope to depict the scene when He shall introduce us to the principalities and powers in heavenly places and bid us sit with Him in His throne, even as He sits with His Father in *His* throne. Surely, then, the holy angels, who have never sinned, will unite in exclaiming, "Behold how he loved them!" In that moment, the least among us shall know more of His love than the greatest of us can ever know while here below. Meanwhile, we have much of the joy of heaven even while we are upon this earth, for as Paul wrote, "God, who is rich in mercy, for his great love wherewith he loved us, even when we were dead in sins, hath quickened us together with Christ, (by grace ye are saved;) and hath raised us up together, and made us sit together in heavenly places in Christ Jesus" (Eph. 2:4–6).

What Some Saints Have Done to Show How They Loved Their Lord

There have been *those who have suffered for Christ's sake*. They have lain in damp dungeons and refused to accept liberty at the price of treachery to their Lord and His truth. They have been tortured but would not yield up their fidelity to God. Hundreds of thousands of brave men and women, and children, too, have faced death in a glorious calm and triumphant with joy while many of those who looked on learned to imitate their noble example, and others who heard their dying testimonies could not help exclaiming, "Behold how these loved their Master!"

Others have shown their love to their Lord by untiring and self-sacrificing service. They have labored for Him, at times, under great privations and amid many perils, some as missionaries in foreign lands and others as workers in our own country. Their hearts were all aglow with love for their dear Lord and Savior, and they spent their whole time and strength in seeking to win souls for Him, so that those who knew them could not help saying, "Behold how they love their Lord!" Some of us can never hope to wear the ruby crown of martyrdom, yet we may be honored by receiving the richly jeweled crown from the hand of Christ as He says to each of His true laborers, "Well done, good and faithful servant;...enter thou into the joy of thy lord" (Matt. 25:23).

Then we may have known *some saints who showed their love to their Lord by weeping over sinners and praying for their conversion.* There have been gracious men and women who could not sleep at night because of their anxiety over the eternal welfare of their relatives and friends, or even of lost ones who were personally unknown to them. They have risen from their beds to agonize in prayer for sinners who were either calmly sleeping or at that very hour adding to their many previous transgressions. There have been others who could not hear a blasphemous word as they passed along the street without feeling a holy indignation at the injury that was being done to their best Friend, and at the same time their eyes filled with tears of pity for the poor blasphemers, and their hearts poured out a stream of supplication for those who were thus ignorantly or wantonly sinning against the Most High. They have been like Jeremiah weeping over the lost, and like Moses and Paul ready to sacrifice their own souls for the sake of others, until men have been compelled to say, "Behold how these weeping and pleading saints love their Lord and love lost sinners for His sake!"

Others have proven their love to their Lord by the way in which they have given their substance to His cause. They have not only given a tithe of all they had to the great Melchizedek but also counted it a high privilege to lay all that they had upon His altar, counting that their gold was never so golden as when it was all Christ's and that their lands were never so valuable to them as when they were gladly surrendered to Him. Alas, that there should be so few, even in the Church of Christ, who thus imitate their Lord, who freely gave Himself and all He had that He might save His people! Blessed will the Church be when she gets back to the Pentecostal consecration that was the fitting culmination of the Pentecostal blessing: "And all that believed were together, and had all things common; and sold their possessions and goods, and parted them to all men, as every man had need" (Acts 2:44–45).

Another admirable way of proving our love to Christ is *by being scrupulously careful to please Him in little things as well as in the more important matters.* One of the worst signs of this present evil age is that so little is thought of even the great things of Christ— His atoning sacrifice, His high priestly character and work, His kingly rule, and so on, while the little things of Christ, those that are less by comparison with these, are often utterly despised. There was a time in Scotland when the men of God signed the Solemn League and Covenant with their blood; how many would do that today? One jewel of Christ's crown, that priceless jewel of the crown rights of the King of kings, was sufficient to call into the battlefield the noblest of Scotland's sons; but today, the very crown of Christ is kicked around like a football by some of His professed servants. He who really loves His Lord will not trifle with the least jot and tittle of His Lord's will. Love is one of the most jealous things in the universe. "God is a jealous God" because "God is love." The wife who truly loves her husband will not harbor even a wanton imagination; her fidelity to him must not be stained even by an unchaste thought. So must it be with every true lover of the Lord Jesus Christ. God grant that we may do our Lord's will so scrupulously in great things and little things and in all things alike that those who see us in our daily life may be compelled to say, "Behold how these Christians love Jesus Christ their Lord and Savior!"

Still, beloved, remember that when our love has reached its climax, it can only be like a solitary dewdrop trembling on a leaf compared with the copious showers of love that pour continually from the heart of our dear Lord and Master. Put all our loves together, and they will not fill a tiny cup, and there before us flows the fathomless, limitless, shoreless ocean of the love of Jesus; yet let us have all the love for Him that we can. May the Holy Spirit fill our souls to the brim with the love for Jesus, for His dear name's sake!